THE GROLIER
LIBRARY OF
World War I

THE GROLIER LIBRARY OF
World War I

1918: A FLAWED VICTORY

Grolier Educational
Sherman Turnpike, Danbury, Connecticut 06816

Grolier Educational
Grolier Publishing Company, Inc.

This edition first published 1997 by Grolier Educational, Danbury, Connecticut 06816.
Copyright © 1997 Marshall Cavendish Limited, 119 Wardour Street, London W1V 3TD, England.

Set ISBN: 0-7172-9065-4
Volume ISBN: 0-7172-7698-8

Library of Congress Cataloging-in-Publication Data

The Grolier Library of World War I.

p. cm.
Includes bibliographical references and index.
Contents: [1] The causes of the war — [2] 1914: The race for the sea — [3] 1915: The lines are drawn — [4] 1916: The year of attrition — [5] 1917: The U.S. enters the war — [6] 1915–1917: The Eastern front — [7] 1918: A flawed victory — [8] The aftermath of the war.
Summary: Covers the causes of World War I, the battles and strategy involved, and the aftermath in chronological format.
ISBN 0-7172-9065-4 (hardcover)
1. World War, 1914–1918—Encyclopedias. Juvenile. 2. World War, 1914–1918—Encyclopedias. I Grolier Educational (Firm).
D522.7.G76 1997
940.3'03—DC2196–50230
CIP
AC
Printed and bound in Italy

Marshall Cavendish Limited
Managing Editor: Ellen Dupont
Project Editor: Tim Cooke
Senior Editor: Sarah Halliwell
Editors: Andrew Brown, Donald Sommerville
Senior Designer: Melissa Stokes
Picture Research: Jeff Cornish, Darren Brasher,
    Ann Hobart-Lang
Editorial Assistant: Lorien Kite
Production: Craig Chubb
Index: Ella J. Skene

Consultant:
Dr. John L. Pimlott,
Head of the Department of War Studies,
The Royal Military Academy Sandhurst,
England.
Text:
Dr. Lloyd Clark, Senior Lecturer,
The Royal Military Academy, Sandhurst.
Dr. Roderick R. McLean,
University of Edinburgh.

CONTENTS

The *Grolier Library of World War I* has many features designed to help you find the information you're looking for quickly and get the most out of the books. This page explains how.

Locator maps Use with the main map on pp. 8–9 or the larger maps within the article to find out exactly where the action is taking place.

Eyewitness Firsthand accounts by soldiers and civilians will help you imagine what it might have been like to live through the war.

Date Line An instant guide to the dates and places covered in the article or what aspect of the war it covers, such as Home Front or Sea War.

Biography Brief lives of most of the major characters of the war, both military leaders (The Commanders) and others (War Profiles).

Alternatives "What if…?" features will help you decide for yourself whether or not the men running the war could have done things differently.

Larger maps show places of particular interest in more detail. With the locator maps at the start of each article, they help you understand where things happened.

Factfiles An at-a-glance summary of each major battle. Because many casualty figures from the war are inaccurate, they are meant as a guide only; they usually include dead and wounded.

Features Highlight interesting aspects of the war and discuss them in more detail. They are grouped in categories: women; weapons; tactics; the home front; new inventions; behind the lines; the armies; men of the future; and politics.

Where to Find Every article ends by telling you where you can find related topics. Use them to read in more detail about different aspects of a subject or to learn how different incidents and people relate to each other.

Maps: Each volume begins with a world map on pages 8–9 to show you the location of the action covered in the book.

Contents: Pages 5–6 of each volume list all the subjects covered in the book, as well as every feature, biography, and background entry. Boxes and biographies are marked in italics; more general background entries are highlighted in bold.

Background Features: These pages, easily found because of their entries' shaded background, deal in detail with important subjects related to the articles they follow.

Glossary & Bibliography: At the back of the book is a glossary that explains words often used in the set. A bibliography lists other books you can read about World World I.

Index: An index that covers the entire set appears in each volume.

1918: A Flawed Victory

In spring 1918 the German army launched a series of offensives on the Western Front that broke the stalemate of the trenches. By the fall, the tide had turned in favor of the Allies, partly because of the arrival in Europe of American troops, who saw their first action at Cantigny.

In Italy the Italians pushed back the Austrians, demoralized by the collapse of their empire from within. A final offensive in Palestine knocked the Ottoman Empire out of the war. Germany itself descended into revolt before the Armistice ended the war on November 11. In Africa, where small groups of soldiers had been fighting in Europe's colonies throughout the war, the last Germans surrendered 12 days later.

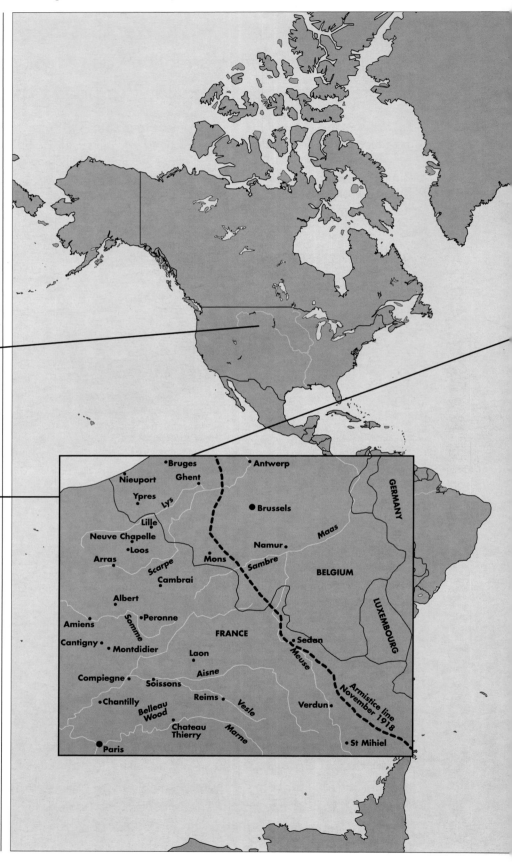

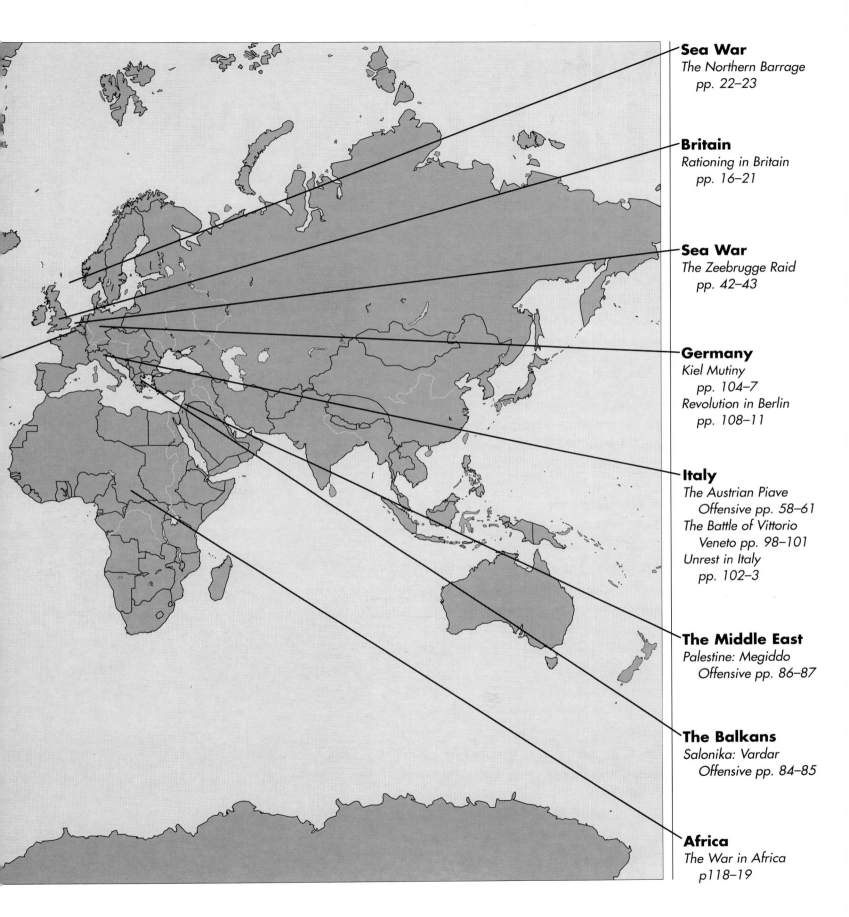

Wilson's
14 POINTS

The U.S. President's idealistic statement of America's war aims became the basis of the negotiations that would bring peace.

I n the early afternoon of January 8, 1918, the president of the United States, Woodrow Wilson, stood up to address a joint session of Congress. Although America had been at war for nine months, this was the first public declaration of the country's war aims. Wilson's speech made Fourteen Points. They were to become the basis for the talks that ended the war and led to the Paris Peace Conference of 1919.

A moral vision

The pressure on Wilson to outline American war aims had been growing for some time. The American people needed reassurance that they were fighting for good moral reasons. The president wanted to provide solid foundations for peace against which proposals from other nations could be judged.

During the fall of 1917 Wilson asked a group of experts – known as "The Inquiry" – to produce a report on the war aims of all the countries in the war and to outline what they thought America's own goals should be. The Inquiry's report formed the basis of the Fourteen Points.

The president's speech was initially well received around the world. Even Lenin, the communist ruler of the new Soviet

Thomas Woodrow Wilson, 28th president of the United States, based his Fourteen Points in part on his belief in a "peace without victories." He thought this would be the best way of avoiding the bitterness that might cause future wars.

The Fourteen Points

1. Open diplomacy; no secret treaty making.
2. Freedom of the seas in war as well as in peace.
3. The removal of all economic barriers.
4. National armaments to be reduced.
5. Colonial disputes to be judged impartially, with equal weight being given to the interests of the subject populations and the claims of the colonial governments.
6. The evacuation by the Germans and Austrians of all Russian territory.
7. The restoration of Belgian sovereignty.
8. All occupied French territory to be restored and Alsace and Lorraine to be returned.
9. Italian frontiers to be readjusted along clearly recognized lines of nationality.
10. The peoples of Austria-Hungary to be given the opportunity for autonomous development.
11. Romania, Serbia, and Montenegro to be restored and Serbia given access to the sea. Balkan interstate relations to be settled on lines of allegiance and nationality.
12. The non-Turkish peoples within the Ottoman Empire to be given the opportunity for autonomous development.
13. The establishment of a Polish state with access to the sea.
14. A general association of nations to be formed to guarantee political independence and territorial integrity to great and small states alike.

Union, applauded its vision. The Points seemed to reflect a desire shared by many people – not just for peace, but for a new beginning. They offered a future in which countries worked together to avoid war and in which different peoples would have a say in how they were governed.

However, it soon became clear that there would be problems implementing some of Wilson's ideas. Criticism of the president began to grow. Some Europeans argued that he did not understand the complexity of European relations. They said that the Points were unrealistic.

Some of America's allies thought that Wilson was trying to dictate what he wanted without consulting them. The economic problems the European countries suffered

Field Marshal Hindenburg (left) and General Ludendorff (right), the virtual military dictators of Germany from 1916 to 1918. They opposed the territorial concessions Germany would have to make under the Fourteen Points but were overruled by the new German civilian government in October 1918.

Passengers being rescued from a French liner, torpedoed by a German U-boat. The freedom of the seas laid out in Point 2 of the Fourteen would have prevented both the U-boat campaign and the British blockade of Germany.

because of the war had helped give the U.S. great financial influence over them. Some European leaders thought that the Fourteen Points, though they sounded idealistic, actually aimed to further American economic interests. Premier Clemenceau of France quipped, "The Good Lord only gave us ten commandments; the American President has given us fourteen."

Each of the major Allied nations found fault with one or more of the Fourteen Points. They were never formally agreed as

alternatives

What if Germany had accepted Wilson's Fourteen Points as the basis for peace in January 1918? The Allies would have been unlikely to do the same. Wilson formulated his points without consulting the British and the French. The plan he came up with contained demands that ran contrary to his allies' interests. Neither Britain nor France accepted Wilson's idealistic program when it was first presented to them. Whatever Germany's reaction to the Fourteen Points, it is improbable that the war could have ended without Allied agreement.

an overall Allied policy, but no matter what Europe's leaders thought, Wilson and his Fourteen Points became hugely popular in every war-weary Allied country.

On October 4 the new German chancellor, Prince Max of Baden, sent a note to Wilson. The Germans were being pushed back on the Western Front and were prepared to make peace on the lines of the Fourteen Points. Wilson had tempted Germany to the peace table on his terms.

But it was still not easy to turn Wilson's idealistic vision into a formal peace treaty. The European countries were embittered by four years of war. Although the Fourteen Points did help end the war in November 1918 and later formed the basis for the Paris Peace Conference, they also stored up problems for the future – problems that would help cause World War II.

WAR PROFILES

Walter Lippmann 1889–1974
American writer
In 1914 Lippmann became editor of the important liberal journal *New Republic*. In 1917 he joined "The Inquiry" and traveled to Europe to coordinate its work with Allied Intelligence agencies. But in 1919 Lippmann criticized the Treaty of Versailles as a catastrophic failure. He said that the peace would not last because President Wilson had allowed the Fourteen Points to become diluted. After the war Lippmann continued his career as a journalist and became famous around the world. He died in 1974.

Polish-American nurses ready to go to France. Point 13 of the Fourteen urged the creation of an independent Poland.

Polish White Cross
for the
Polish Army in France

Daily Life in the U.S.A.

The American people were united in their support for the war, even though it had brought many changes to their lives.

Women from Boston proudly show off a pile of peach stones collected for the war effort. The stones were used to make filters to go into gas masks.

T he popular mood in the United States in 1918 was intensely patriotic. Former president Theodore Roosevelt summed it up when he said, "He who is not with us, absolutely and without reserve of any kind, is against us, and should be treated as an alien enemy." President Wilson's Fourteen Points had given focus to American war aims, and people threw themselves into the war effort. Government propagandists in the Committee of Public Information ran cam-

paigns to keep support for the war solid and make sure that all Americans were "doing their bit."

Many people joined voluntary organizations such as the Red Cross. Many more helped finance the war by buying War Savings Stamps and Liberty Bonds. Even when the rate of income tax was raised, few people protested. People did not complain when they were asked to eat less

Mexico desert – and abandoned without food and water.

The enthusiasm for the war lay partly in a government-sponsored hate campaign against the enemy. However, this also resulted in a backlash against German-Americans which the authorities did little to stop. German books were removed from libraries, and spy fever swept the country. People were encouraged to report on their

Hunters in Michigan show off the deer they have killed. Hunting was described as patriotic because it helped conserve food supplies.

wheat, meat, and sugar in order to help the Allies beat food shortages in the early months of 1918.

With the majority making sacrifices, anyone who seemed not to join in – such as antiwar politicians or members of labor unions – were treated with contempt. Draft dodgers and "slackers" were hounded. Radical spokesmen were sent to prison. In Arizona, more than 1,000 strikers were rounded up and transported into the New

neighbors. False stories were told of uprisings in cities, such as Milwaukee and Cincinnati, with large German-American communities. There were even rumors of pro-German saboteurs putting glass in bandages being sent out to the troops.

Most of the rumors were nonsense. The fear they created, however, did bring the European war closer to the American people. This only strengthened the resolve of the American people to continue the fight.

WHERE TO FIND...

Wilson's 14 Points: 7:10

Red Cross: 5:68

Liberty Loans: 5:64

Anti-German Feeling: 5:62

Wobblies: 5:60

Fear of Espionage: 5:57

Rationing in
BRITAIN

As the German U-boat war threatened to bring Britain to her knees, the government had to take drastic measures.

A propaganda poster encourages the men and women at home to be strong during the food crisis created by German U-boat attacks.

By 1918 any remaining enthusiasm in Britain for the war had died. The previous year had been one of increasing hardship at home and military disappointment at the front. Everyone was weary of the war. Even now, after four long years, no end to the fighting was in sight. Most of all, people were scared. Food was growing scarce.

As an island Britain relied heavily on food and other essential materials being imported by sea. But from the beginning of the war German U-boats, or submarines, had ruthlessly targeted British trade routes. With submarines sinking incoming ships, supplies could not get through. After four years of this campaign Britain was on the brink of starvation.

London in desperation
The winter of 1917 and 1918 saw food shortages all over London. Lines steadily grew outside stores. During January and February the capital's police counted some 500,000 people standing in lines every Saturday. Often there were so many people that husband and wife took turns to wait on freezing sidewalks for several hours at a time. In London, *The Times* newspaper reported the increasingly chaotic scenes: "The food queues [lines] continue to grow. Outside the dairy shops of certain multiple firms in some parts of London women begin to line up for margarine as early as five o'clock on Saturday morning, some with infants in their arms, and others with children at their skirts."

There were shortages of margarine, tea, sugar, and especially meat. The govern-

By the King

A PROCLAMATION

GEORGE R.I.

WE, BEING PERSUADED that the abstention from all unnecessary consumption of grain will furnish the surest and most effectual means of defeating the devices of Our enemies, and thereby of bringing the War to a speedy and successful termination, and out of Our resolve to leave nothing undone which can contribute to these ends or to the welfare of Our people in these times of grave stress and anxiety, have thought fit, by and with the advice of Our Privy Council, to issue this Our Royal Proclamation, most earnestly exhorting and charging all those of Our loving subjects the men and women of Our realm who have the means of procuring articles of food other than wheaten corn as they tender their own immediate interests, and feel for the wants of others, especially to practise the greatest economy and frugality in the use of every species of grain, and We do for this purpose more particularly exhort and charge all heads of households

TO REDUCE THE CONSUMPTION OF BREAD IN THEIR RESPECTIVE FAMILIES BY AT LEAST ONE-FOURTH OF THE QUANTITY CONSUMED IN ORDINARY TIMES . . . .

TO ABSTAIN FROM THE USE OF FLOUR IN PASTRY AND MOREOVER CAREFULLY TO RESTRICT OR WHEREVER POSSIBLE TO ABANDON THE USE THEREOF IN ALL OTHER ARTICLES THAN BREAD
. . . .

Given at Our Court at Buckingham Palace this Second day of May in the Year of Our Lord 1917 in the Seventh Year of Our Reign.

GOD SAVE THE KING

NOW WE THE UNDERSIGNED MEMBERS OF THIS HOUSEHOLD HEREBY PLEDGE OURSELVES ON OUR HONOUR TO RESPOND TO HIS MAJESTY'S APPEAL

Dorothy A. Wright
Bruce S. Wright
Beatrix F. Wright
Arthur S. Wright

A royal proclamation dated May 2, 1917, urging the British public to eat less bread and use less flour. By 1918 it became clear that voluntary measures like this were not enough. Compulsory rationing was introduced instead.

ment tried to get people to buy alternatives to meat such as eggs, or fish such as sprats and herring, but the meat shortages continued. Soon, the government ordered Londoners to go without meat for two days a week.

The government hoped that it would not be necessary to bring in rationing. But at the same time they feared that the people would become demoralized by constant shortages. To encourage Londoners, the government put up propaganda posters around the capital which declared, "Eat Slowly. You Will Need Less Food," and, "Keep Warm. You Will Need Less Food." But people were still hungry and the shortages got worse. It was even illegal to feed bread to the birds along the Thames River.

The situation reached crisis point and the government had no choice. It began

rationing in London and surrounding areas in February 1918. By the end of April the system covered the whole country. People now had to produce ration cards in order to buy meat and fats such as butter, margarine, and lard. Each person was allowed only 15 ounces of meat, five ounces of bacon, and four ounces of fats per week. The government hoped that by limiting the amount of food people could buy, there would be just enough to go around and no one would go without. Hoarding food attracted a heavy fine. Nobody could afford either to waste or share food. Cooks had to think up new recipes.

But to everyone's relief, the desperate measure of rationing soon had results. In the spring of 1918 the long lines outside shops began to dwindle. By the summer the threat of starvation had passed.

A German submarine emerging from the depths. The main cause of rationing in Britain was its enemy's policy of sinking supply ships bringing food to the island.

Using substitute foods

With basic foods in short supply, cooks had to use substitutes that they could get more easily, such as root vegetables that were grown in Britain, rather than varieties that had to be imported. This often made for rather strange recipes:

home front

Turnip Jelly:

Cook 8 oz turnips in a little water until a smooth pulp. Cook 1 lb sliced cooking apples in $^1/_4$ pint of water until a smooth pulp. Mix the turnip and apple pulps together. Measure this and add 1 lb sugar for each 1 pint of pulp. Put back into the saucepan, stir until the sugar has dissolved, then boil until stiffened.

This jelly never becomes as firm as the real fruit jelly.

Carrot and Seville Orange Marmalade:

Wash and squeeze $1^1/_4$ lb of Seville oranges. Cut up the peel and place it, with the juice, in a large basin with 2 pints of water. Leave to stand overnight. Next morning, simmer gently until the peel is tender. Remove the seeds.

Cook 2 lb of carrots in a pint of water until soft, and then mash them. Add the carrot pulp and water to the oranges and bring to the boil. Add 2 lb of sugar and boil the mixture rapidly until it thickens.

As this marmalade contains so little sugar, unlike real marmalade, it will not keep longer than a week.

Pages from a British ration book.

Spanish Flu Pandemic

A woman breathes through a sophisticated, but useless, flu mask in 1919. The flu pandemic was a shattering conclusion to four years of war. Many soldiers returned home to find their families had been wiped out by the merciless virus.

In the fall of 1918, as exhausted, demoralized soldiers began to limp their way home, another catastrophe hit the disbelieving world. A deadly influenza virus swept the continents with terrifying speed. Millions of people died around the globe.

No one knows precisely where the pandemic, or worldwide epidemic, began. The French and others believed that it came from Spain and called the disease Spanish Flu. As one doctor noted, "It came like a thief in the night and stole treasure." With little warning, it struck down the young and the old, the rich and the poor. It emptied entire classrooms and factory floors in a matter of days.

The influenza was particularly deadly when contracted by children and young

A masked workman disinfects a British bus with an antiflu spray, March 2, 1920.

adults. About a quarter of all those who died were 15 or under; nearly half were under the age of 35.

In the United States 550,000 died; in Britain 228,900; in Germany 225,330; in France, 166,000; and in India a phenomenal 16 million people perished.

Once infected, the chance of recovery was slim. Fine gauze masks and antiseptic sprays were used to try to stop the spread of the infection, but they were largely useless. Because no one knew the precise nature of the virus, no vaccine could be prepared. Doctors could prescribe no other treatment but rest.

In total, the Spanish influenza killed 20 million people – double the number who died in the war itself.

An American policeman wears a gauze mask to protect against flu infection in 1919. Such masks had no practical benefit.

WHERE TO FIND...

Sinking of the Sussex: 4:38

Submarine Campaign: 5:18

The Northern BARRAGE

The Allies laid thousands of mines between Britain and Norway to prevent German submarines reaching the Atlantic.

United States battleships on maneuvers with the British fleet in the North Sea. From December 1917 American battleships served as part of the British Grand Fleet, keeping guard over the North Sea.

The Northern Barrage was a massive Allied minelaying effort designed to stop German submarines from passing from their home bases to the Atlantic Ocean to hunt Allied shipping.

Since the beginning of the war the British had tried to stop the U-boats from reaching the Atlantic shipping lanes by blocking the Straits of Dover with minefields and patrol boats. By the spring of 1918 they had finally succeeded. From May 1918 the German naval command ordered all U-boats on their way to the Atlantic from German bases to pass around Britain to the north.

The idea of laying a minefield that would block this route was first suggested by the U.S. Navy early in 1917. But it was not until Admiral Mayo, commander of the Atlantic Fleet, raised it at the inter-Allied

A depth charge from a U.S. patrol vessel explodes near a suspected U-boat.

THE COMMANDERS

**Henry Mayo
1856–1937
American admiral**
Mayo was commander in chief of the Atlantic Fleet when the United States entered the war. In August 1917 President Wilson sent him to London to advocate the use of a convoy system that would help safeguard merchant shipping from German submarine attack. Mayo wanted to produce new antisubmarine measures rather than improve existing equipment. In particular Mayo was an advocate of the Northern Barrage. He was probably the most able admiral in the United States Navy during World War I.

conference in September 1917 that Allied leaders seriously considered the plan.

It was some months before the actual minelaying could begin because of the massive resources that were required. The gap to be covered was 250 miles wide. It was estimated that about 100,000 mines would be needed to form an effective field.

American factories made the mines since British industry was already stretched to the limit with other war production. Trains brought the mines to a loading depot in Virginia, and 21 cargo ships took them from there to Scotland.

Allied ships began laying the western sector of the field on March 3, 1918, with the eastern and central sectors following, beginning on June 8. By October 1918 a minefield 35 miles wide in some places had been established. About 70,000 mines were actually laid by the end of the war.

The British doubted whether the Northern Barrage was worth its $40 million dollar price tag. The mines were not very reliable and it was quite easy for the German submarines to find gaps. By the armistice the minefield had destroyed only six U-boats, even though German submarines passed through the barrage area in increasing numbers.

Despite great American enthusiasm for the project, the Northern Barrage was of limited effectiveness and did little to influence the outcome of the war.

The KAISERSCHLACHT

On a foggy morning in March 1918 the Germans began a major offensive in northern France. They believed that ultimate victory in the war against the Allies could soon be theirs.

Right: German stormtroopers practice an attack. The Germans used new infantry tactics for their attacks in 1918. Stormtroopers were trained to infiltrate between Allied strongpoints and cut them off to be captured later by other German forces. This proved to be a very effective technique.

Far right: British and French troops prepare to defend an improvised position during their retreat from the German attack.

FactFile

OPPOSING FORCES	German: 1,000,000	British: 505,000
		French: 204,000
COMMANDERS	Chief of Staff: Ludendorff	C. in C.: Haig
	2nd Army: von der Marwitz	3rd Army: Byng
	17th Army: von Below	5th Army: Gough
	18th Army: von Hutier	
LOCATION	60-mile front southeast of Arras, northern France	
DURATION	March 21 – April 5, 1918	
OUTCOME	Germans advance 40 miles but cannot turn tactical victory into strategic success.	
CASUALTIES	German: 250,000	British: 178,000
		French: 77,000

By early 1918 the German army was in a perilous position. Although the war on the Eastern Front had ended, German submarines had failed to knock the British out of the war. And large numbers of U.S. reinforcements were due in France.

General Ludendorff, the German supreme commander, came up with a solution – a major offensive in France that would inflict a decisive defeat on the Allies before the Americans could arrive.

The offensive, codenamed Operation Michael, began on March 21, the Kaiser's

EYEWITNESS

As the bombardment that heralded the Kaiserschlacht began, a British artillery captain, Arthur Behrend, was asleep in his dugout:

66 I awoke in a start to find that everything was vibrating; the ground, the dugout, my bed. There was a crash and my door was blown of its hinges and the room was filled with the smell of high explosives. I sat in bed powerless to move – in any case one might just as well be killed decently in bed instead of half naked while struggling to get into one's shirt. 99

birthday. In the Emperor's honor, the Germans named the assault *Kaiserschlacht*, or "the Kaiser's battle." Three German armies attacked along a 60-mile front south of Arras. The British, Ludendorff thought, would retreat toward the Channel ports of France. The Germans had an overwhelming advantage in manpower. The attackers outnumbered the defenders almost three to one.

A massive bombardment

The Germans began their attack in the early hours of a foggy morning. Nearly 6,000 German guns opened fire on the British positions. In the most concentrated

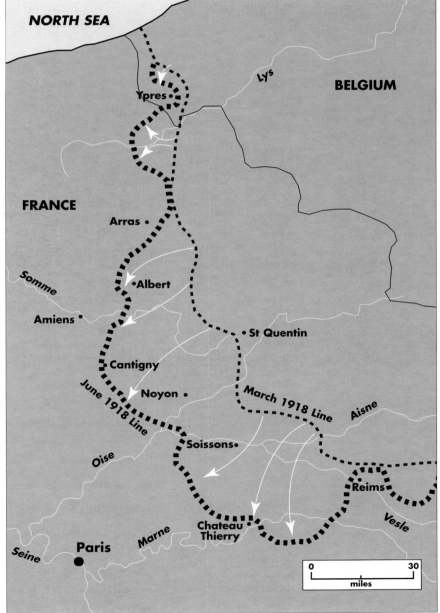

British troops at work on repairing their trenches to strengthen them against the German attack.

artillery bombardment the world had ever known, thousands of mortars and gas shells fell on the British for more than five hours.

When the bombardment lifted, small groups of German stormtroopers – trained for just such an assault – moved across No Man's Land, the deserted area between the German and Allied lines, under cover of the fog.

Their advance was swift, particularly in the south. Soon the British front line had fallen and Ludendorff's troops were surging forward. By nightfall the British were in full retreat, having lost 20,000 prisoners. The Kaiser's birthday had gone well.

In the days that followed, the Germans continued their overwhelming onslaught. To the north of the line, around Arras, the British somehow managed to contain the attack. To the south, however, they suffered great losses and had to retreat further. In their haste they failed to destroy bridges and roads, allowing their pursuers to follow quickly. By March 25 the Germans had advanced 25 miles. They now threatened Amiens, an important Allied center.

A change of plans

Despite their spectacular territorial gains the Germans had fallen short of achieving their objective, a decisive victory. Now Ludendorff tried to exploit his unexpected advance. He ordered his armies to fan out. One would strike at Amiens, while another was to continue attacking in the north. The third, however, was to turn its attention toward the French capital, Paris.

Crisis for the Allies

The Germans' success caused panic in Allied High Command. The British asked the French for reinforcements; the French refused. Their own troops were weak and vulnerable. And they could not spare the men defending Paris. As the arguments continued, the battle raged on.

Only full Allied cooperation could avoid a major defeat. An emergency conference of Allied generals and politicians on March 26 gave French Marshal Foch overall charge of the Allied forces. In April he became Allied supreme commander on the Western Front. Now, as his first act, Foch sent French troops to help the British at

German advance and slowly began to recapture territory.

The German offensive now slowed down along the entire front. Although Ludendorff attempted to launch a new attack near Arras in the north, the operation had lost momentum. Many of his troops were exhausted. The muddy terrain seriously hampered the easy transport of reinforcements and supplies to the new front line.

Operation Michael was effectively dead. Ludendorff had put everything into the

German troops hauling their guns forward to accompany their attack, March 23, 1918.

Amiens despite the opposition of his French generals.

The decision proved to be a good one. By early April the fall of Amiens appeared imminent: the Germans were on the high ground overlooking the town. With the arrival of French reinforcements, however, the Allies counterattacked. They halted the

offensive. Although it had brought the greatest territorial advances for the Germans since 1914, it had cost the German Army 250,000 casualties. It had also failed to provide the decisive victory that Ludendorff wanted. He decided to try again to the north in Flanders, where he launched the Lys Offensive on April 9.

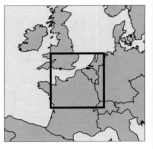

The PARIS GUN

Germany's superguns bombarded Paris from more than 75 miles away. The guns were a remarkable technical achievement – but they were also another step toward total war.

The "Paris gun" being prepared for tests on the firing range.

Just as people in the French capital of Paris were preparing for work on the chilly morning of March 23, 1918, a German shell smashed down on the city. The event caused panic in the French capital and marked a new stage of the war. The city's air defenses had protected it from air attack for three years. But this shell came not from an aircraft but from an artillery gun more than 75 miles away. Never before had a city so far from the front come under artillery fire.

It had taken the German arms company Krupps two years to develop the new weapon, dubbed "Wilhelm's Gun" in honor of the kaiser. Because the guns were developed in secret and demolished after the war, no one knows how many were made. They were enormous and had to be mounted on railroad cars to be moved. The barrels were 112 feet long and had a caliber, or internal diameter, of nearly 8½ inches. On their journey the shells reached an altitude of 24 miles.

The first gun was placed in a forest just behind the German lines, carefully camouflaged so that it could not be seen from the air. At 7:16 a.m. on March 23, 1918, the first

days there may have been more than one gun in use. In total the "Paris gun" – or guns – probably fired 367 shells. One of the worst attacks came on Good Friday, March 29, when Parisians were crowded into church. Just as the priest finished his sermon, the congregation in the Church of Saint-Gervais on the rue Miron heard a dull explosion. The church shook and the roof and part of a wall collapsed. A shell

1918

MARCH–AUGUST

Western Front

Preparing shells for a German long-range gun.

shell began its journey toward Paris. Another 21 shells fell on the city the same day. Stores closed and the streets became deserted. Germany's great spring offensive had just begun and the shelling was doing its job of adding to the confusion in the Allied ranks.

The bombardments continued, with interruptions, for five months. On some

had hit the church. Some 75 people were killed and 90 injured.

On August 9 the last shell fell on Paris. The city had suffered 256 deaths and some 620 injuries. But on the front line the Allied advance threatened to discover the mighty guns. They were taken back to Germany, where they and their secrets were destroyed.

WHERE TO FIND...

Krupp: 1:15
Kaiserschlacht: 7:24
Zeppelin Raids: 3:38
Gotha Raids: 5:74

Heavy Artillery

A German railroad gun blasts away at the Allied lines. Each rail gun was accompanied by its own train, carrying the gunners, ammunition, and all the materials they needed to build their firing position.

World War I was largely an artillery war (see page 3:14). Artillery caused a majority of the casualties in the war – far more than machine guns, rifles, gas, or any other class of weapon.

Heavy artillery could smash opposing defensive positions, create gaps in the barbed wire, and destroy the enemy's gun batteries. The shells tore up trees, wrecked buildings, and churned up the ground. They left the battlefields cratered and empty. But above all else, artillery made the trench soldiers' lives a misery. Bombardments, perhaps lasting a week or more, sapped men's courage and will to live. Sleep was almost impossible. Even if a shell did not hit a trench directly, it could collapse it and bury the inhabitants alive. Flying pieces of red-hot, jagged metal – called shrapnel – could take a man's head off. At any time, even in the quietest part of the front, artillery could bring sudden death or hideous wounds from an unseen enemy 10 or more miles away.

In 1914 all modern armies had many fairly mobile field artillery weapons.

They fired smallish shells – about 3 inches in diameter and 15 pounds in weight – designed to throw out shrapnel when they exploded. This made them very effective against troops in open ground. Such shells, however, lacked the power to smash defenses or the range to hit enemy gun batteries. The armies soon realized that they needed more heavy weapons.

At the start of the war the German army was better equipped with heavy guns than the Allies. Their biggest guns fired a one-ton shell almost 10 miles. Other types could fire 630-pound shells twice that distance. By 1918 the German army had 8,000 heavy guns.

In 1914, by contrast, the Allies had few heavy guns suitable for battlefield use. Most were installed in fortresses. The British and French soon expanded production. They lagged behind for the first years of the war but by 1918 they had caught up with the Germans.

Bigger, more powerful guns brought new problems. Heavy artillery was big, weighty, and clumsy. Special positions had to be built for every weapon so that the guns did not simply drive themselves into the ground as they fired.

Before the war most guns were pulled by horses but now trucks and tractors moved the massive weapons. The biggest guns of all were mounted on railroad cars. By 1918 the French alone had 400 superheavy rail guns. Am-munition supply was another problem. Guns fired millions of shells before every big battle later in the war.

The impact of heavy guns on World War I was huge. A British soldier described a barrage in 1914 as "something worse than the mouth of hell." By 1918 the soldiers had to endure so much more artillery fire that even that horrible experience seemed trivial.

French artillerymen prepare a rail gun for action. Rail guns usually could not be swung around on their mountings, so special curved sections of rail track were built at their firing positions to provide enough maneuverability for aiming.

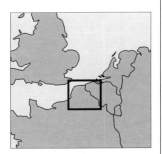

Offensive on the
LYS RIVER

Ludendorff's second attempt to break through Allied lines would lack impact while critically weakening his own forces.

American troops take cover behind a railroad line on April 11, 1918. Some American troops joined the British and French in holding off the German attacks in the first half of 1918. Most of the U.S. forces, however, were still being trained.

FactFile

OPPOSING FORCE	German: 595,000	British: 435,000
COMMANDERS	Ludendorff	Haig
LOCATION	A 12-mile sector extending from the Ypres salient south to Armentières	
DURATION	April 9 – 29, 1918	
OUTCOME	British forced to abandon gains made during 1917, but Germans fail to achieve their objectives.	
CASUALTIES	German: approx. 110,000	British: approx. 110,000

After the failure of the *Kaiserschlacht* – the German spring offensive of 1918 – supreme commander General Erich Ludendorff looked for a new place to break the Allied lines. He chose the Lys River in Flanders, at the northern end of the Western Front. Operation Georgette, the codename for the second German assault of the year, won initial success. But it dealt a fatal blow to the Germans' power and morale.

EYEWITNESS

A British captain guarding the bank of the Lys recalled how the Germans attacked; he was captured in his attempt to fall back from the river:

66 They threw bridges over the Lys, and they just mopped up those two front line companies, wiped them out. Well, they were nearly all new little boys out from England, only been out a few days, only heard rifles fired on the ranges.... They were annihilated, either bayoneted or shot. We were shooting from our little shell hole ... we still had the order 'Hold on at all costs. No retirement.' 'But,' we thought, 'the battalion is nearly wiped out and there's only five of us. Let's get on to this road and run like Hell back to our own troops.' 99

THE COMMANDERS

**Ferdinand Foch
1851–1929
French commander**
A soldier in the French army from 1870, Ferdinand Foch came to prominence before World War I as a theorist rather than a fighting man. His belief in the power of the offensive contributed to the heavy casualties in the 1914 campaigns on the Western Front.

But Foch displayed his generalship while commanding the Ninth Army in the Battle of the Marne, after which he helped to coordinate Allied efforts in northern France and Flanders. In 1917 he was appointed chief of staff to the French Army. A year later he was promoted to overall commander of Allied armies on the Western Front.

Foch worked with Sir Douglas Haig during the successful offensives on the Western Front during the fall of 1918. He headed armistice negotiations in November, imposing harsh terms on Germany.

Ludendorff wanted to keep the pressure on the Allies. Although the *Kaiserschlacht* offensive on the Somme had not broken the Allied lines, it had been a great tactical success. Now the general intended to advance to the rail center of Hazebrouck, then push on to Dunkirk on the Channel coast. He intended to crush the British armies in France.

Operation Georgette opened on the morning of April 9, 1918. Thick mist hung over the battlefield. The Germans began an artillery barrage that went on for 36 hours. Under its cover infantry attacked the left flank of the British First Army along a narrow 12-mile front east of the Lys River. The attack met with instant success. It quickly shattered a demoralized

A British field gun in position for the defense of a canal bridge at St. Venant during the Battle of the Lys on April 13, 1918.

THE COMMANDERS

Erich Ludendorff 1865–1937

German general

Ludendorff was a fairly junior German general in 1914 but rose to prominence quickly during the first few months of World War I. By November 1914 he was chief of staff of the supreme command in the east under Field Marshal Paul von Hindenburg. A successful partnership developed between the two men. They pushed the Russians back in a series of successful battles through the summer of 1916.

In August 1916, when Hindenburg replaced Falkenhayn as head of the German army, Ludendorff became his chief of staff with the formal title first quartermaster-general. Ludendorff became the dominant military and political figure in Germany for the remainder of the war. He governed as a virtual dictator. His failure to win a decisive victory in the west during the spring of 1918, however, led to his forced resignation on October 26.

Portuguese division, pushing it back four miles. British units retreated, too, suffering heavy casualties. Next day Ludendorff threw more men into the attack. They soon recaptured land that the British Army had taken the previous year. By April 12 the Germans had created a gaping 30-mile hole in the British lines.

For the second time in 1918 the British faced a crisis. Field Marshal Douglas Haig, supreme commander of the British troops in France, had few reserves. Most of his troops were still fighting the end of the German offensive on the Somme. In desperation Haig begged reinforcements from the French commander, Marshal Foch.

Haig was determined. He issued a famous order: "Every position must be held until the last man. There must be no retirement. With our backs to the wall and believing in the justice of our cause, each one must fight to the end."

The British managed to resist the German thrust on the Lys. The British Second Army withdrew to better defensive positions. Only a week after Haig's order, it was clear that the German attack was losing steam. The British brought the enemy to a halt at Meteren at the foot of an imposing hill called Mount Kemmel.

Ludendorff strikes again

The Germans had lost momentum. To get the offensive moving again Ludendorff attacked the Belgians beyond Ypres. The assault failed. On April 24, however, another diversionary attack further south, near Amiens, captured the town briefly but was

German stormtroopers advance through the captured town of Bailleul in April 1918. This was one of the furthest points the German attack reached.

A French armored car supports British troops on the Lys at Meteren on April 16, 1918.

pushed back. On the Lys the Germans took Mount Kemmel, but Operation Georgette was virtually over. Two days later Ludendorff tried to advance again but failed. On April 29 he officially called off the battle.

The British had blunted the German army's morale. Ludendorff's men were disillusioned. The offensive had demanded more hard fighting and sacrifice. But it had achieved little except to create an awkward salient, or bulge, in the German line. Now it would be even harder to defend.

Most fatally, Ludendorff had weakened his army. In little over a month he had lost about 350,000 men. They could not be replaced. The Allies had lost fewer men – about 305,000 – but they would be replaced by the American troops landing in France. Unlike Ludendorff, Haig could look ahead with new confidence.

alternatives

What if Marshal Foch had not replaced Pétain during the *Kaiserschlacht*? The German spring offensive put so much pressure on the British and the French armies that Pétain thought about severing links with Haig to leave the French to cover Paris and the British to guard the coast. The move could have had devastating consequences for the Allies. If Foch had not replaced Pétain, the British and French would have had no mutual support and reinforcement. They would have left themselves open to concentrated German attacks that would probably have knocked them both out of the war.

Death of the
RED BARON

The fighters of the air were admired as glamorous heroes living dangerous, exciting lives – and dying brave deaths.

The best known fighter pilot of World War I is probably the German ace Manfred von Richthofen, better known as the "Red Baron." He was named for his red aircraft and his aristocratic blood. But in April 1918 the baron's reign would come to a dramatic end.

Baron von Richthofen's apartment is decorated with number plates from enemy planes he had brought down. Many of Richthofen's fellow pilots found the baron's souvenirs gruesome.

A ruthless hero

Born in 1892, Richthofen began the war in the cavalry before transferring to the air service in 1915. In September 1916 he shot down his first enemy aircraft – a victory that fighter pilots called a "kill." By the following January Richthofen already had 15 victories to his credit. He soon became Germany's leading ace and a national hero known as the "ace of aces."

Richthofen was well known not only for his superb flying skill and fighting tactics, but also for his lack of mercy: he tried to obtain a souvenir from each of his victims' aircraft. In July 1917 he was wounded in the head and put out of action for a time. By the end of the year, however, the German had still managed to score a devastating total of 63 kills. He added steadily to his total the next year.

Early on April 21, 1918, Richthofen took to the skies with his fellow pilots, intending to add to his total of kills, which now stood at 80. The German Fokker planes soon engaged two British reconnaissance aircraft photographing the German trenches over the Somme River. But Canadian fighter pilot Roy Brown spotted the

attack. He led eight Camel planes to try and help the spotter planes, slower and less well armed than the fighters. Among Brown's squadron was a novice. It was Lt. Wilfred May's first aerial action. Brown told the young man to stay on the fringes of the fighting, but the eager May soon found himself in the thick of things. Despite his lack of experience, May dived down on a Fokker and opened fire. The long burst of fire did not trouble the German aircraft – but it did succeed in jamming May's own guns. With no way to defend himself, May could not stay where he was. He disengaged and headed home.

His departure did not go unnoticed. The keen-eyed Richthofen followed the lone

Air War

Manfred Freiherr von Richthofen, the "Red Baron," poses for the camera.

plane. May only learned that Richthofen was on his tail was when the Red Baron's machine guns opened up and peppered his fuselage, the body of his plane. Panicked, May sent his aircraft into emergency evasive action, swooping, diving, and swerving to shake the German off, but to no avail. The chase continued above the Somme River, as Richthofen used all of his experience to wear his opponent down.

Just as Richthofen was about to go in for the kill, Captain Brown appeared on his tail. In a flash, Brown's machine guns rattled, hammering holes into Richthofen's red fuselage. The Fokker swerved out of control before gliding awkwardly to the ground. The aircraft came to a juddering halt two miles behind the British lines.

WAR PROFILES

**Edward Mannock
1887–1918
British fighter pilot**
Edward Mannock transferred to the Royal Flying Corps from the Royal Engineers in August 1916, despite being virtually blind in one eye. After arriving in France in April 1917 Mannock had very little combat success for a couple of months. His tactics tended to be cautious but he had a raging hatred of the enemy.

Then, in one three-week period, Mannock shot down six enemy aircraft. He was awarded a medal and promoted to captain and flight commander in July 1917. By the following summer Mannock had added another 36 victories to his credit.

Mannock died on July 24, 1918, when a bullet from the ground ignited his fuel tank. Mannock recorded 73 official kills, although his true tally was probably much higher. His Victoria Cross, Britain's highest award for bravery, was awarded posthumously in July 1919.

The funeral procession of the Red Baron on April 22, 1918. The Allies buried the pilot with full military honors.

WAR PROFIILES

Albert Ball
1896–1917
British fighter pilot

At the outbreak of war, Albert Ball joined the infantry, but he transferred to the Royal Flying Corps in 1916. In May he joined a fighter unit. He recorded his first victory in July. A month later he attacked five German aircraft single-handed, driving down three of them.

Odds meant nothing to Ball: He took risks and thought only of attack. One of his favorite tactics was to attack the enemy head-on, wait until the German lost his nerve and swerved, and then shoot him down.

Ball was last seen entering dense cloud in combat with a German fighter on May 7, 1917. He had scored 44 victories. Publicity made him the first British pilot to become a national hero. After his death he was awarded a Victoria Cross medal for his bravery.

In most crash landings a pilot would quickly jump out of his aircraft in case it blew up. But on this occasion there was an ominous stillness. Eventually a few people approached the Fokker. They found Richthofen slumped over his controls, his head resting on his guns. The Red Baron was dead. He had been shot through the chest.

Although the kill was awarded to Brown, nobody can be certain that it was his guns that did the fatal damage: both an Australian machine-gun company and an artillery brigade also claimed to have fired the shots from the ground. Nonetheless on April 22 it was the British who dropped a message to the Germans at their fighter airfield. It read: "To the German Flying Corps. Rittmeister Baron Manfred von Richthofen was killed in aerial combat on April 21, 1918. He was buried with full military honors. From the British Air Force."

The German population was deeply saddened by Richthofen's death. The hero's body was transferred to a German war cemetery after the war, but in 1925 it was removed and laid to rest in Berlin.

Hermann Göring

Hermann Göring was one of the best German air aces of World War I, with 22 kills. But he is better known as one of Hitler's key men in the Nazi regime during World War II.

Göring trained as a soldier but eventually went to the Western Front as an air observer. By October 1915 he had qualified as a pilot and joined a fighter squadron. Singled out for his initiative and iron will, Göring was placed in command of the squadron in May 1917. He took part in the great air battles that preceded the German offensives of March 1918, where he developed brave and intelligent new tactics.

Hermann Göring in his Fokker triplane fighter ready for a patrol over the Western Front..

Göring eventually took command of Richthofen's old formation in July 1918. Although by then the Germans were losing the air battle, fighting with old aircraft and little fuel, Göring led with distinction until the armistice. In 1935 Göring became commander of Hitler's Lüftwaffe, or air force. A born leader with a forceful personality, he was one of the most important members of the Nazi Party. He killed himself during the Nuremberg war crime trials in 1946 by taking poison in his cell.

men of the future

WHERE TO FIND...

Fighter Planes:
  4:102
Fokker: 5:43
Nazism: 8:96

The Air Aces

American ace Eddie Rickenbacker in his Spad fighter plane.

Edward Rickenbacker 1890–1973 American fighter pilot

Although he became the American ace with the highest number of kills, Rickenbacker only became a pilot in 1918. Before the war Rickenbacker had been a successful motor racing driver. Although he spent some time as General Pershing's driver, the determined Rickenbacker learned to fly in his own time and set his sights on becoming a fighter pilot.

In March 1918 he joined the 94th Aero Squadron, United States Army Air Service, scoring his first kill on March 29. He was an ace within a month.

By the end of the war Captain Rickenbacker was commander of the 94th. By the armistice he had 26 confirmed kills to his credit. He returned home a national hero and was awarded the Medal of Honor in recognition of his bravery and services.

World War I was a young man's war, and nowhere more so than in the air. A pilot might be considered a veteran in his early 20s. The young men who joined the air service had to learn extremely quickly if they were not to be shot out of the skies. Even in 1917 pilots were sent to duel in France after only 17 hours of solo flying.

The most successful fighter pilots were described as "aces." To become an ace, a pilot was only required to have five confirmed kills. Yet there were relatively few of them – pilots did not live long. Because combat flying was so new and dangerous, the aces were seen as something very special. People regarded flying as romantic; the air war seemed much more glamorous and exciting than the stagnant trench warfare on the ground. The public loved the handsome, dashing aces, who quickly became national heroes. With each new tale of heroism and daring victory, the aces boosted the morale of men, women, and children back home.

When they were killed, however, the public felt a terrific sense of loss. The death of Manfred von Richthofen, the Red Baron, for example, had a devas-tating effect on the German public. General Ludendorff, the German supreme commander in 1918, said that Richthofen's death had a psychological impact on Germany equivalent to the loss of about 30 divisions – about 300,000 men.

After April 1917 the emphasis in air combat changed from the solitary ace to tactics of team effort. Now "packs" would overwhelm the lone flyers. The age of the ace was largely over.

German soldiers gather round a crashed French airplane on the Western Front in 1918.

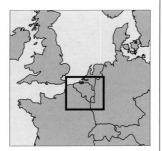

The ZEEBRUGGE RAID

In April 1918 Britain tried to block U-boat harbors in Belgium in a surprise nighttime raid. The attack was bravely carried out but it did not succeed.

In 1918 British leaders were desperately worried by the shipping losses caused by the German U-boats. There were major U-boat bases in occupied Belgium, particularly at the ports of Zeebrugge and Ostend. The British decided to block these ports by sinking old ships in the harbor entrances. The raids took place on the night of April 22, 1918. The daring plan and the bravery of the attackers were reported around the world. In Britain it had a special significance because the next day, April 23, is St. George's Day, dedicated to England's patron saint. But the raids were not successful. The harbor at Zeebrugge was only partly blocked, and the attack on Ostend failed completely.

then deliberately sink them inside the narrow harbor entrance. The sunken ships would prevent any German submarines that were at sea from returning to the port. Any that were already in the harbor would be trapped there.

The plan

The Zeebrugge base was a tough target. A long curving pier, or mole, protected the harbor entrance. The Germans had fortified the pier with guns and searchlight batteries. The British plan had two parts. First, an old cruiser – *Vindictive* – and other smaller ships would attack the pier, putting ashore a landing party of 700 Royal Marines. Meanwhile, three more old ships would take advantage of the diversion to sail past the pier. Their crews would

The battered British cruiser Vindictive pictured after her return from Zeebrugge. The mats and shields on her decks and superstructure were meant to protect the landing parties from German fire but failed to do so.

An aerial view of Zeebrugge after the operation. The passing tug shows that the sunken ships did not block the channel.

THE COMMANDERS

**Roger Keyes
1872–1945
British admiral**
Keyes was one of the most aggressive British naval commanders of the war. He was always involved in planning new ways of striking at the Germans.

In 1914 Keyes commanded British submarines and took part in the Heligoland Bight operation. In 1915 he served at Gallipoli as naval chief of staff. Keyes tried to persuade Admiral Carden to renew bombardment operations after the first attempt failed.

In October 1917 Keyes became director of plans at the British Admiralty. He thought up and led the Zeebrugge raid.

Under the cover of darkness the small British flotilla approached its target. But the raid did not start well. In the face of fierce German defense the Royal Marines from the *Vindictive* lost three-quarters of their men killed or wounded. The ship itself was badly shot up. The gun batteries on the harbor mole remained untouched.

When the three ships of the blocking force headed for the inner harbor, they came under heavy fire. One ran aground before reaching the target and had to be abandoned. Despite the enemy fire the other two were successfully sunk at the narrowest point of the channel but did not block it completely. U-boats and small surface ships could still pass by.

Although the raid failed, it provided a much-needed morale boost for the British. Many people actually thought that it had worked because the German submarine campaign soon became less effective. The reasons for that, however, lay elsewhere.

WHERE TO FIND...

Naval Blockade:
2:52; 3:44

Sinking of the Sussex: 4:38

Submarine Campaign: 5:18

Heligoland Bight:
2:46

FRANCE

Oise

Somme

Cantigny

Front Line
May 27

Aisne

Soissons

Reims

Marne

The Third Battle of the
AISNE

The Germans needed a decisive victory on the Western Front to end the war. But when their commander, Ludendorff, became too greedy, his attack ground to a halt.

German stormtroopers leave their trench to begin an attack. The stormtrooper units had been specially trained earlier in 1918. They had heavy casualties in the German attacks in 1918, which greatly weakened the whole German army.

FactFile

OPPOSING FORCES	German: 697,000	French: 195,000 British: 60,000
COMMANDERS	1st Army: von Below 7th Army: von Böhn	French 6th Army: Duchêne
LOCATION	A 30-mile sector from Noyon to Reims	
DURATION	May 27 – June 6, 1918	
OUTCOME	The Germans gain ground but do not achieve goals.	
CASUALTIES	German: approx. 100,000	French: approx. 98,000 British: approx. 29,000

The Germans' offensives of March and April 1918 – the *Kaiserschlacht* and the attack at the Lys River – had brought them no strategic advantage. Ludendorff had dealt the British army a severe blow, but he still needed a decisive victory in the west. And with American troops steadily pouring into France, he had to act quickly. So in May the Germans launched their third offensive, aiming to set the Allies up for a final blow.

Ludendorff had clear aims for the attack. He knew that the British army was the strongest of his enemies but he was also aware that French reinforcements had been crucial to the British during the previous German offensives. He now intended to cripple the French army before making a final attack against the British in Flanders. His order issued on May 1, 1918, made this clear: "This attack has the objective of disturbing the present united front of the Entente [Allies] … and thereby creating the possibility of a victorious continuation of the offensive against the British."

A cunning plan

The German supreme commander chose a ridge near the Aisne River, topped by the famous Chemin des Dames road, as the place for the attack, which was codenamed Operation Blücher. He knew that the Allies had been lulled into a false sense of security there: Both sides regarded this area, between Reims and Soissons, as a quiet sector where troops could rest; even now, three battle-weary British divisions were doing just that. The area was lightly defended by units of French General Duchêne's Sixth Army, with a further nine divisions in the rear. The Germans, attacking with two complete armies, would have a six-to-one advantage in manpower.

Operation Blücher began at 1:00 a.m. on May 27 with a massive artillery bombardment along a 24-mile front. Then, just before first light, the German infantry rose out of their trenches and attacked the Allied positions. The bombardment had hit

An American heavy artillery battery in position near Ploisy, on the Aisne front, on July 20, 1918. Various American units strengthened the Allied front during the Aisne battle.

German troops cross a broken bridge over the Aisne Canal on June 10, 1918, as they try to continue their advance.

THE COMMANDERS

Louis Franchet d'Esperey 1856–1942

French general

Franchet d'Esperey was promoted to take command of Fifth Army on the eve of the Battle of the Marne in September 1914. By 1917 he was the highly regarded commander of France's northern group of armies. But his standing was badly dented when, in May 1918, the German offensive in the Chemin des Dames sector pushed his troops back 20 miles.

As a result he was removed from the Western Front to take command of the Allied forces on the Salonika front. Later in 1918 Franchet d'Esperey redeemed himself by launching a major offensive that forced the Bulgarians to seek an armistice.

In 1922 he was promoted to Marshal of France.

the Allies with such ferocity that the Germans were slowed more by the churned-up ground than by a forceful enemy defense.

Flawed tactics

The army group commander Franchet d'Esperey unwittingly contributed to the disaster. This French officer favored massing his troops in forward defense rather than using "defense-in-depth" tactics: staggering his forces at prepared positions. This meant that the German artillery and assault troops who stormed the Chemin des Dames Ridge easily cracked his front line and destroyed the Allied center almost immediately. By 9:00 a.m. on the first day of the offensive Ludendorff's troops had reached the Aisne River.

Despite these early successes, however, the Germans could not turn the Allied retreat into a rout. Although the Germans forced their enemies back toward Soissons,

the French did not disintegrate, and the British divisions put up enough resistance to prevent the German front from widening too far. Still, by the end of the first day the Germans had advanced ten miles – the biggest movement on the Western Front since trench warfare began in 1914.

At dawn on May 28 the German attacks continued. Duchêne grew increasingly desperate. The French general's Sixth Army had already suffered massive casualties, and the troops now lacked sufficient firepower to slow the enemy. The Germans had destroyed most of the French machine guns and field artillery with their bombardment, and seized what was left as they advanced. On the second day of the offensive the Germans took another five miles. The situation looked increasingly bleak for the Allies.

At this successful point in the push the German supreme commander became more ambitious. Ludendorff increased the

tactics

Defense in depth

By the end of August 1916 the Germans abandoned their policy of defending and regaining ground at all costs. Instead, they used defense-in-depth tactics, an extremely effective method of trench warfare.

The aim of defense in depth was to create a lightly held forward zone up to two and one half miles deep, consisting of an almost continuous line of outposts. Behind this area would be a row of strongpoints designed to dislocate and disorganize an enemy attack. The main line of resistance came in the battle zone, which was between one and two miles deep. This area was heavily entrenched and had dense belts of barbed wire that channeled attacking infantry into the fire of waiting machine guns. The bulk of protective artillery was positioned here to bombard the enemy. Finally, there was a rear zone where the reserves were kept, out of the range of enemy fire.

By 1918 the British and French armies were also adopting this system, although they had not fully put the tactics into practice by the time of the German offensives.

A French machine-gun team join British troops in an improvised defensive position on May 29, 1918.

weapons

Flamethrowers

In 1916 the Germans attacked French soldiers at Verdun with one of their most formidable weapons, flamethrowers. French soldiers saw German soldiers approaching with tanks strapped to their backs. These contraptions threw forward a powerful jet of burning liquid. To their horror the French saw oily black flames reaching toward their trenches. Now, along with being shot or gassed, the Allies could be burned to death.

At first, the flame-thrower took the French completely by surprise, both terrifying and demoralizing them. But they soon realized these early flamethrowers were flawed: their range was only about 40 yards. The soldier with the flame-thrower had to get very close to the enemy to use it effectively.

By the time of Aisne offensive flamethrowers were in common use. But French soldiers found a way to counter them: they realized that firing a bullet into the flamethrower tank turned the German attacker into a flaming torch.

Right: A German flamethrower team in action.

Far right: A group of weary British and French prisoners of war captured by the Germans during the Aisne offensive. By May 30, 1918, the Germans had taken some 50,000 Allied prisoners, together with 800 guns.

objectives of the offensive. The purpose of Operation Blücher was no longer merely to wear down the French army. It was now to push toward the valuable prize that had eluded the Germans in 1914 – the French capital, Paris, which temptingly lay just 80 miles to the southwest.

To achieve this glorious goal, General Ludendorff urgently needed more rein-forcements for his front line. The prospect of gaining a decisive victory persuaded him to call up the reserves that he had been saving for a future attack against the British in Flanders.

Meanwhile, German troops had reached the Marne River at Château-Thierry by May 30. But their momentum was beginning to slow. The Allies were responding to the attack. And to counter the threat to the French capital, Allied commanders rushed two American divisions into the area to help to stem the German advance. The U.S.

cipline was beginning to crumble in certain units. On June 6 Ludendorff had no choice but to call the offensive to a halt.

Again the Germans had failed to turn tactical gains into strategic success. Since late March their offensives had done little but create three bulges in the Allied line: in the north, between Ypres and La Bassée;

1918
MAY-JUNE
Western Front

2nd Division arrived at Meaux, northeast of Paris, on May 30, and covered the road to the capital. The U.S. 3rd Division, meanwhile, took up a position along the Marne River a few days later.

By the time that the first of these American troops had been deployed, Ludendorff's Operation Blücher was in desperate trouble. German losses were heavy, their lines of communication were being stretched to breaking point, and dis-

in Picardy, between Arras and Compiègne; and now to the south, between Soissons and Reims. The Germans had taken ground but not broken their enemy, despite good preparation and carefully crafted surprise. The Allies had managed to hold on, though their commanders would not: Duchêne lost his job, while d'Esperey was transferred to Salonika. The German army was now close to exhaustion, creating an ideal moment for the Allies to strike.

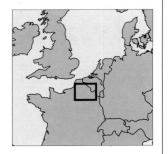

CANTIGNY

The Battle of Cantigny was the first attack mounted by American forces in France. It was a small advance, but a significant sign of what was to come.

In late May 1918 German troops were surging forward in their offensive on the Aisne. The Allies were in retreat, and the Germans threatened the French capital, Paris. Just then a small but successful American attack to the west of the Aisne at Cantigny helped to raise Allied spirits. It also showed what the growing American forces in France might accomplish in the months to come.

Americans in the front line

During late April General Robert Bullard's American 1st Division occupied a sector of the front west of Montdidier, where it was serving as part of the French army. Bullard's men were the first American division to enter the line on an active battle front. The newly arrived Americans were eager to prove themselves in action.

Directly in front of 1st Division's new position, high on top of a hill, lay the vil-

Right: American infantrymen pick their war forward through barbed wire toward the German defense lines. One of the group has already been hit by enemy fire.

FactFile			
OPPOSING FORCES	German: 20,000		American: 14,000
COMMANDERS	Von Hutier		Bullard
LOCATION	Western Front, west of Montdidier		
DURATION	May 28 – 31, 1918		
OUTCOME	Americans capture and hold the village of Cantigny. Although not strategically significant, the first U.S. victory is an important morale boost for the Allies.		
CASUALTIES	German: approx. 6,500	American: approx. 1,800	

lage of Cantigny. Cantigny was held by Prussian General Oskar von Hutier's veteran Eighteenth Army. The village gave the Germans excellent observation positions, while the high ground screened activity in their rear areas. In mid-May the 28th Infantry Regiment of Bullard's 1st Division was ordered to take Cantigny.

The 28th Infantry carefully rehearsed its plans over similar terrain behind their lines for several days before the attack. American and French artillery, machine guns, mortars, tanks, flamethrowers, and engineering units would support the infantry, along with two more American companies. During the night of May 27 Bullard's troops waited anxiously for the dawn, and their chance to prove themselves in battle.

The attack begins

The Allies launched their assault early on the morning of May 28, the second day of the German offensive taking place on the Aisne River to the east. As the American infantry advanced, all the raw soldiers' nervousness disappeared. The troops'

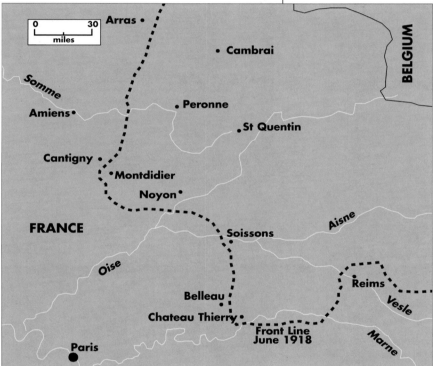

minds were set firmly on their objectives. The Germans resisted tenaciously, but the well-rehearsed attackers were too strong. In just a few hours Bullard's troops took the village, together with 200 prisoners. But their job was not over yet.

Having taken Cantigny, the Americans prepared to defend themselves against the inevitable German counterattacks. They dug trenches, laid barbed wire, and con-

American troops played an important part in halting the German advance in May to July 1918. Americans fought especially at Cantigny, Château-Thierry, and Belleau Wood.

THE COMMANDERS

Robert Bullard
1861–1947
American general

Bullard was an able and popular field commander but had little opportunity to show his expertise on the battlefield before the armistice.

Bullard was appointed to command the U.S. 1st Division in late 1917. He gained a good reputation both for his division's success at Cantigny in May 1918, and for his role as commander of III Corps in the Second Battle of the Marne from July to August 1918.

In October 1918 Bullard was rewarded with the command of the newly created U.S. Second Army in the Meuse-Argonne sector of the Western Front. His troops saw little fighting there before hostilities ceased in November.

Far right: The blank face of a captured British soldier shows the classic dazed expression of shell shock.

Right: A wounded U.S. Marine is given first aid in a front-line trench before being evacuated to a hospital.

EYEWITNESS

An American private, Paul Wright, saw his first action at Cantigny:

66 The noise was incredible – the guns, the rifles, the blasts, the shouting and the screaming. I was nervous but soon forgot about it as we began to move forward. I could see the village in front of me and hoped to heaven that my legs would get me there. … At one point we had to stop for a rest. I dropped down into a shell hole and found myself looking at a headless torso. 99

structed strongpoints as the first German shells began to fall at noon. A ferocious artillery bombardment supported repeated German infantry attacks that lasted for the next 72 hours.

Von Hutier's Eighteenth Army fought hard to retake the ground they had lost and break the morale of the inexperienced American defenders. But everything they tried failed. By the end of May 31 the exhausted German troops had no choice but to concede defeat. The Americans had not only taken their objective; they had successfully defended it, too.

The Battle of Cantigny was a small one compared with some of the large-scale engagements fought previously on the Western Front. It cost less than 200 lives, although there were also more than 1,000 Americans wounded.

But the victory at Cantigny had a great psychological impact. It boosted the Allies' morale at a time when they were struggling to contain the repeated German offensives of the spring. It also proved to the other Allies, Britain and France, that if they could only hold out a little longer, a large and powerful American army would soon be in action beside them. Even veteran German troops would find this new force difficult to withstand.

behind the lines

Shell shock

During World War I no soldier could stay at the front for more than a few weeks without his mental state being affected and his military efficiency declining. Many thousands of soldiers suffered from a form of mental injury known then as shell shock. This was caused by the strain of life at the front, and especially by long enemy bombardments. Symptoms included trembling, tearfulness, and damaged memory.

The problem was a difficult one for all armies. The British medical services, for example, reported about 20,000 cases in 1915 – nine percent of battle casualties.

At first shell shock victims were treated as cowards; some were even sentenced to death and executed. But gradually improved medical knowledge meant that shell shock was recognized as a psychiatric problem. Later in the war rest and counselling resulted in 87 percent of British psychiatric casualties returning to the front within one month. Yet, despite measures like these, many hundreds of thousands of veterans suffered long-term psychiatric disorders.

Shell shock is now also known as battle fatigue. Modern doctors believe that battle fatigue will eventually affect every soldier, however brave, who spends a long period in combat.

BELLEAU WOOD

The United States Army's first large battle of the war taught the troops on both sides many lessons.

American troops set up a Lewis machine-gun position in a quickly dug trench.

FactFile

OPPOSING FORCES	German: 50,000	American: 27,500
COMMANDERS	7th Army: von Boehm	2nd Division: Bundy
LOCATION	Western Front east of Paris, 8 miles west of Château-Thierry	
DURATION	June 6 – 25, 1918	
OUTCOME	Americans clear Belleau Wood after three weeks of fighting.	
CASUALTIES	German: 20,000	American: 8,800

In the last days of May and early June 1918 Allied reserves from all over the Western Front rushed to meet the continuing German attacks. But there were signs that the German plans were going astray. In early June near the Marne River east of Paris, at Belleau Wood, United States troops not only halted the German advance but pushed it back as well.

The United States 2nd Division was mainly composed of U.S. Marines. They

EYEWITNESS

Captain George Hamilton, commander of the 49th Company, 1st Battalion, 5th Marine Regiment, remembers his advance toward Belleau Wood:

66 I have vague recollections of urging the whole line on, faster, perhaps, than they should have gone ... of snatching an iron cross ribbon off the first officer I got – and shooting wildly at several rapidly retreating Boches [Germans]. Farther on, we came to an open field – a wheat-field full of red poppies – and here we caught hell.... It was a case of every man for himself. **99**

arrived in the sector on June 1. At first they had to repel a number of German attacks. Soon they were ready to go on the offensive themselves.

The Marines advance

Before dawn on June 6 Belleau Wood and the village of Bouresches, a few hundred yards east, were bombarded by French and American artillery. The barrage was inaccurate, however, and stopped too soon.

The Marines advancing to Belleau Wood itself lost many casualties to the German machine guns as they attacked across the open fields without artillery support. They made few gains and the assault ground to a halt.

Meanwhile, the attack toward Bouresches had problems of its own. The stone-built village was a veritable fortress with overlapping fields of machine-gun fire providing excellent protection.

German prisoners captured by the Marines at Belleau Wood are escorted into captivity.

American infantry creep forward to raid a German position early in 1918. The men do not carry rifles but are equipped with bags of hand grenades, more useful in short-range trench battles.

Throughout June 6 American troops tried advancing on the buildings in line and sniping at their windows, but had to give up and wait until nightfall to attack again. By creeping up on the village and then charging with bayonets, the Marines eventually took Bouresches at 2:00 a.m. on June 7.

The few Marines who had managed to reach the trees in Belleau Wood in the initial push had to stay hidden there all night. When they advanced again at first light on June 7, they were immediately cut down by German machine-gun fire.

Renewing the attack

With the Germans so firmly fixed in their defensive positions there was nothing else to do. The only option was to restart the stalled offensive. A 200-gun artillery bombardment was planned for June 9. For the next two days the tired Americans tried to establish themselves in the devastated wood, but without success. On June 12 an even larger concentration of guns hammered the area, followed by an attack by fresh troops. This time the Americans did clear the fringes of the wood, but it took nearly two weeks more and a 14-hour bombardment to clear it completely.

For both the Americans and the Germans the battle was a learning experience. The American troops and their leaders learned just how hard it was to take a well-defended enemy position, but the Germans learned that they now faced a brave and tenacious new opponent.

The U.S. Marines

When the United States declared war on Germany on April 6, 1917, the elite U.S. Marine Corps numbered just under 14,000 men. During the war the Marine Corps increased in size to 75,000 men but its standards were never lowered. On June 14, 1917, the first contingent of Marines (the 5th Regiment) set sail from the United States for France. During the course of the war approximately 30,000 Marines were sent overseas to fight in France with the American Expeditionary Force; 3,284 of them never returned.

Marines pose for the camera at a training camp. Marine recruiting posters claimed that the German nickname for the Marines was "devil dogs," a tribute to their aggression in battle.

The Marines fought with bravery, skill, and tenacity during 1918 and scored many important victories over more experienced opponents. The contribution made by the Corps during the last six months of the war in battles such as Belleau Wood and the Meuse-Argonne Offensive only served to enhance the high esteem in which the Marines were already held around the world.

WHERE TO FIND...
The U.S. Enters the War: 5:26
Meuse-Argonne Offensive: 7:88
Cantigny: 7:50

The Austrian
PIAVE OFFENSIVE

In the summer of 1918 Austria made a last effort to defeat Italy. The ambitious offensive only added to the disintegration of Austria's already weary armies.

Austria's generals thought that 1918 presented them with an opportunity to settle defeat Italy once and for all. The previous year the Italian army had been humiliated in the Battle of Caporetto. Since then the Austrians had been strengthened by the arrival of troops from the east, where they had been fighting the Russians. But the Austrian leaders did

FactFile			
OPPOSING FORCE	Austrian: 850,000	Italian: 750,000	
COMMANDERS	Chief of General Staff: Arz von Straussenburg	Chief of General Staff: Diaz	
LOCATION	To the north of Venice, Padua, and Verona along a line following the Piave River and then west toward Lake Garda		
DURATION	June 10 – 22, 1918		
OUTCOME	The Austrians fail to knock Italy out of the war as they intend and fatally damage their own offensive capability for the future.		
CASUALTIES	Austrian: approx. 70,000	Italian: approx. 85,000	

Right: Heavy artillery moves along a narrow mountain road in the upper part of the Piave Valley. The difficult terrain made it hard to use artillery effectively.

not realize how well the Italians had recovered from the defeat at Caporetto. Instead of winning a glorious triumph the Austrian generals fought a battle that only added to the stresses that were already tearing the Austro-Hungarian armies apart.

After Russia made peace at Brest-Litovsk in March 1918, Germany remained committed to ending the war with a decisive military victory. To help them in their aim the German leaders tried to persuade the Austrians to send some troops to the

Western Front, but the Austrians decided to attack Italy instead.

The success over the Italians at Caporetto made the Austrians optimistic that one final great push would crack their enemy wide open. The renewed Austrian confidence, however, merely masked a dangerous complacency. Their army was not the force that it had been in October 1917 and many senior officers severely

underestimated their enemy. They also misjudged their own men. By the spring of 1918 the Austrian army was deteriorating fast. Its levels of equipment, supplies, and manpower were low and it was clearly in no fit state for a major offensive.

The Italians on the other hand had bounced back quickly from their defeat. They spent early 1918 building new, strong defensive positions. The Italians had lost many weapons at Caporetto, but the other Allies had now supplied replacements from their plentiful production.

The Austrian plan

At first the Austrian generals disagreed on a plan for the offensive. The chief of the general staff, Arz von Straussenburg, eventually decided on a pincer movement. General Boroevic's army group was to begin the offensive with an advance across the Piave River toward Padua in the coastal sector. General Conrad would then join the attack further inland and attack from the Trentino district toward Verona.

The opening moves

The offensive began on June 10 when Boroevic's Fifth and Sixth Armies advanced from between Montello and the sea and quickly crossed the Piave. After advancing some five miles on a 15-mile

Below: The Italian defenses on the Piave River included artillery positions set up on floating rafts.

men of the future

Ernest Hemingway

Hemingway was born on July 21, 1899, in Oak Park, Illinois, and became a journalist with the *Kansas City Star* after leaving school.

When America entered the war, Hemingway desperately wanted to fight but failed his army medical because of bad eyesight. Hemingway joined the American Red Cross instead.

In April 1918 Hemingway was sent to Italy as an ambulance driver. He was severely wounded during the Piave River offensive. He was hit by two bursts of

machine-gun fire as he went to help a fallen comrade. Hemingway had to spend the next three months in a hospital.

After World War I Hemingway resumed his career as a writer. One of his finest novels, *A Farewell to Arms*, published in 1929, draws heavily on his wartime experiences in Italy. Hemingway was to become one of the greatest writers of the 20th century but, after a life of great domestic upheaval, he committed suicide in July 1961.

front, Boroevic thought that the Italian army was ready to collapse. He was wrong. For the next eight days there was ferocious fighting as the Italians counterattacked.

By June 19 Boroevic's situation was desperate. The river rose because of heavy rain and this, combined with bombing attacks by British aircraft, destroyed most of the pontoon bridges bringing his supplies across the Piave. By June 21 the Italians had turned the Austrian flank and the next day they pushed Boroevic back.

Meanwhile General Conrad's Tenth and Eleventh Austrian armies began an even less successful advance on June 15. By the second day of the offensive Italian, British, and French troops had halted Conrad's progress and were launching a strong counterattack. Within a week Conrad's men had suffered 40,000 casualties.

The offensive was a disaster for the Austrian army. Their defeat was so complete that it put the Austrians into a period of shock that was soon followed by a rapid drop in morale. Failure at the Piave River accelerated the decline of the Austrian army: Instead of crushing the Italians, it had precisely the opposite effect.

A British ambulance makes its way along a muddy road at Salonika, in Greece. Mud and rain were just as big a problem when it came to getting the wounded to a hospital as they were for the men at the front line.

behind the lines

Evacuating casualties

Life in the medical services during World War I was dangerous and very stressful. Stretcher-bearers had a particularly hazardous job. Although unofficial local truces were sometimes made so that both sides could collect their wounded, more often than not they had to be gathered under fierce enemy fire.

Many stretcher-bearers and ordinary soldiers won medals for their bravery in rescuing casualties. Ironically, some of these brave men were those who had refused combat service for conscientious or religious reasons.

The wounded men faced a difficult journey to aid posts and hospitals. In muddy conditions it might take six men to carry a stretcher – difficult and exhausting work.

The severely wounded had to be taken back to mobile hospitals behind the lines by motor or horse-drawn ambulance, but their ordeal was still not over. Roads were often shelled and usually muddy and uneven. The casualties would be bounced about cruelly throughout the long, slow journey since the ambulances did not have good springs or suspension.

WHERE TO FIND...

Caporetto Offensive: 5:100

Treaty of Brest-Litovsk: 6:112

Vittorio Veneto: 7:98

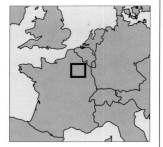

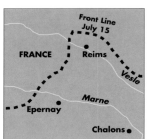

Men of a German stormtrooper detachment pose with their machine guns during the Second Battle of the Marne.

The Second Battle of the MARNE

At the Marne Germany's 1918 offensives ran out of steam. Instead Allied counterattacks began. They would not end until the German army had been defeated.

In early July 1918 the Germans were still on the advance in France. Germany's General Ludendorff planned yet another diversionary attack to draw the Allied reserves from northern France. He hoped that after victory on the Marne a new offensive against the British in the north would knock them out of the war.

This would prove to be Ludendorff's last attack of the war because this time the Allies were ready. They quickly halted the German attack and retaliated with a far more successful advance of their own.

Opening moves

The Second Battle of the Marne began on July 15 when four German armies attacked from around Reims with the aim of pushing southward toward Chalons and Château-Thierry. The German First and

French in this sector were now also using the "defense-in-depth" system, holding their main forces back out of effective artillery range so that they would be ready to counterattack. Together with their spoiling bombardment this meant that the German attack did not get very far. By 11:00 a.m. on the first day the advance towards Chalons was halted.

Meanwhile on a 22-mile front to the west of Reims the German Seventh and Ninth armies were having more success.

FactFile

OPPOSING FORCES	German: 850,000	Allied: 500,000
COMMANDERS	Supreme commander: Ludendorff	Supreme commander: Foch
LOCATION	From Chalons in the east to Soissons in the west	
DURATION	July 15 – August 6, 1918	
OUTCOME	This German offensive turns into a French counter-attack that forces Ludendorff to retreat. The Allies regain the strategic initiative.	
CASUALTIES	German: approx. 168,000	Allied: approx. 108,000

Third Armies advanced on a 26-mile front, but the soldiers were not as confident of success as before. Many of the specially trained stormtroopers who had spearheaded the German attacks earlier in the year had been killed. Their replacements were inexperienced and less aggressive. Many German infantry units were now also badly understrength.

French intelligence had even discovered the time and place of the attack. To disrupt the German preparations the French artillery bombarded the German lines shortly before the attack began. The

The French Fifth Army had not learned how to defend properly against the German attacks. It had too many troops in its forward positions that were easily pounded by the German artillery. The Germans smashed two Italian divisions serving with the French and managed to get their leading units across the Marne.

Ludendorff thought that victory was at hand. He was so sure that the French were crumbling that he ordered the heavy guns in northern France to begin preparations for his long-planned attack against the British. But Ludendorff was wrong.

Above left: A French artillery observation team watches the effect of their fire on the German lines near Reims. One member of the team has tapped into the telephone wires running along the trench to send instructions to the guns.

The Second Battle of the Marne **63**

THE COMMANDERS

Charles Mangin 1866–1925
French general

Mangin was one of the most aggressive French commanders of the war. Ordinary soldiers serving under him disliked him. They called him "the Butcher" because so many men were killed in the attacks he planned. Mangin said that high casualties were inevitable whatever he did and that attacking was the only way to win the war.

Mangin played a crucial role at Verdun in 1916. In 1917 he was one of the few senior officers who supported the Nivelle offensive. He was dismissed after it failed.

In 1918 Mangin was back in favor and in July, as commander of Tenth Army, he led the first major Allied offensive of the year during the Second Battle of the Marne.

Right: Gas masks were not just useful for military purposes. This American soldier is using his to make peeling onions a little more comfortable.

Far right: A British sentry rings a gas warning bell, near Ypres in 1916. Units at the front would always have a gas sentry on duty to sound a warning if a gas attack was suspected.

behind the lines

Antigas measures

Although the first large gas attack at Ypres in 1915 found the Allied soldiers entirely unprepared, countermeasures were soon in production. Within a week 300,000 gas helmets had been made. These consisted of a gauze rag soaked in sodium thiosulphate, held between the teeth and tied behind the head. From 1916 all the major armies introduced respirators which included filters to remove the gases from the air the soldier was breathing and a mask to protect the eyes.

These respirators gave good protection, but it was crucial to put them on promptly. Every small section of trench would have a gas alarm, to be sounded as soon as gas was detected.

Gas masks were uncomfortable and very tiring to wear. They always reduced a soldier's fighting effectiveness. By 1918 effective gas masks meant that gas was causing comparatively few casualties. Commanders on both sides continued to use gas as a weapon, however, because they knew that having to wear gas masks would hamper the enemy troops so much.

An American field artillery crew during a rapid fire barrage. One gunner throws aside the case of the shell that has just been fired before reaching for new ammunition.

On July 17 the French Ninth Army stopped the Germans from exploiting their bridgehead over the Marne. The next day the Allied troops struck back.

The Allied counteroffensive

At 4:35 a.m. on July 18 a French barrage crashed down onto German positions to the west of Château-Thierry. The French Sixth Army moved up close behind to take full advantage of the devastation that had been caused. The attacks were led by 346 tanks. The fresh and eager American 1st and 2nd Divisions were among the assault troops. Then, 45 minutes later, the French Tenth Army surprised the Germans with an advance toward Soissons.

By noon the French had moved forward four miles. By the evening they had captured 15,000 prisoners and 400 guns. Further important advances were made in the south of the salient by the French Fifth and Ninth armies.

The counterattack panicked the Germans. They were not expecting to have to fight a defensive battle. On the night of July 19 and 20 the Germans retreated across the Marne River. The Allied advance continued and soon German communications between Château-Thierry and Soissons were threatened.

Ludendorff's troops were pushed out of Soissons on August 2 and by the following day they had fallen back to the Vesle and Aisne rivers. The Allied counterattack was eventually brought to an end on August 6 when it was clear that the enemy was once again securely entrenched.

Ludendorff's plans had failed. On July 20 he had admitted that the planned offensive in the north was now impossible. The German army was exhausted after four and one half months of continuous attacks. By early August the Allies could look to the future with hope. The military initiative was now theirs.

WHERE TO FIND...

Battle of the Marne: 2:54
Ludendorff: 7:34

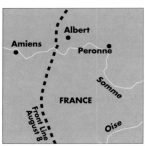

AMIENS

The opening battle of the Allies' counteroffensive on the Western Front would turn the tide of the war, shattering the morale and will of the German army.

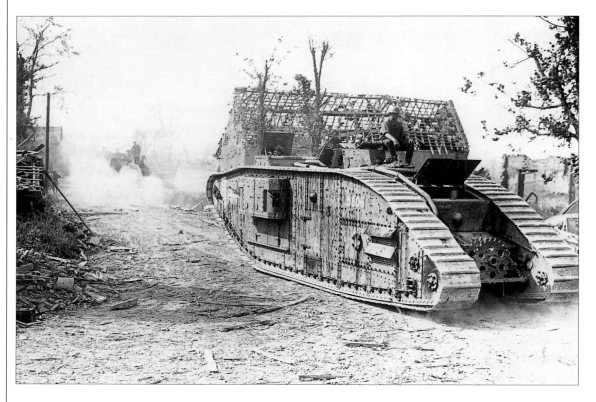

British tanks advance during the Battle of Amiens. Some tanks, like the one nearest the camera, were armed only with machine guns; others carried heavier cannon as well.

FactFile

OPPOSING FORCES	German: 2nd and 18th armies	British: 4th Army French: 1st Army
COMMANDERS	von der Marwitz, von Hutier	British: Rawlinson French: Debeney
LOCATION	Amiens, northern France	
DURATION	August 8 – 15, 1918	
OUTCOME	Allied victory marks the turning point of the war.	
CASUALTIES	German: 40,000	British: 22,000 French: 24,000

General Erich Ludendorff, the effective military ruler of Germany, gave August 8, 1918, a name that stuck. He called it "the black day of the German army." An Allied assault east of the French city of Amiens broke the spirit of the enemy. The battle marked a turning point in the war.

The Allies' original aim was more modest. They wanted to secure the railroad that linked Amiens to Paris from German artillery bombardment. On August 8 Australian and Canadian troops spearheaded the attack. The odds were on their side. They had the crucial support of 500 tanks. Overhead flew British aircraft, supporting the infantry with guns and bombs. Just as importantly, the pilots supplied vital information about German movements and the state of their defenses.

The Allied success was spectacular. On the first day alone Canadian troops advanced six miles, taking 12 villages and capturing large numbers of prisoners and guns. French and British troops made similar gains. After only three days, the Allies had captured 24,000 prisoners – a huge number compared with earlier battles.

The Germans were floundering. When they brought in reinforcements to stop the breakthrough, the Allies added more French troops to their attack, and continued to make gains. By the time their advance came to a halt in mid-August they had recovered much of the ground lost in the German March offensive.

The German will was weakening. During the battle some troops surrendered without much of a fight. Others accused comrades who wanted to fight hard of prolonging the war unnecessarily.

A kilted Scottish soldier guards two German machine gunners he has taken prisoner.

German artillery fires as rapidly as possible to try to halt the Allied advance.

It was not just the German soldiers who were losing the will to fight. Their leaders were also coming to accept that the war must be ended. After the Allies' success at Amiens Ludendorff himself was forced to admit that Germany could no longer win the war. Kaiser Wilhelm reached the same conclusion. "We have reached the limit of our capacity," he told Ludendorff, "the war must be ended."

A plea for peace

On August 14 Germany's ruling Crown Council met at Spa, in Belgium. Ludendorff – shaken by the defeat at Amiens – advised his colleagues to begin immediate peace negotiations. Other senior army commanders shared his view. They feared that Germany's military position would only deteriorate further as thousands of fresh, well-equipped American troops flooded into France to join the Allies.

But the war was not over. The German leaders still refused to contemplate unconditional surrender. Until they did, their soldiers had no choice but to fight on.

Allied troops collect weapons and other equipment salvaged from the battlefield. In the background a battalion medical post gives first aid to wounded men before they are sent further back to the hospital.

WHERE TO FIND...

Recuperation

The armies of the First World War depended on manpower. They could not afford to lose trained men to injury or mental problems. After a battle doctors and nurses simply patched up any casualties who could fight on and sent them back to the front.

Wounded men were treated in field hospitals, where conditions were often chaotic and dirty. Several operations would be going on simultaneously. Doctors might carry out as many as ten amputations in an hour. A wounded soldier described his impressions of such a hospital. He was shocked by the "constant flow in and out of the operating room of desperately wounded men, the screaming when dressings were changed on the stump of an arm or a leg recently amputated, a head gashed up, part of a face blown away, or a stomach punctured; the insane gibbering, mouthing, and scorching profanity of men partially under ether."

Despite such conditions many soldiers spoke highly of the skill of the doctors who treated them, and appreciated the care and attention which they received from the nurses. Indeed many wounded soldiers enjoyed their stay in hospital, glad to be rid of lice-ridden clothes and freezing, wet trenches.

Many thousands of men, however, needed more serious treatment. High velocity bullets and flying chunks of metal from artillery shells caused hideous wounds and loss of limbs. Poison gas filled men's lungs with choking fluid or blinded them. The trenches were full of disease, caused by the filthy conditions that encouraged lice, rats, mosquitoes, and flies.

Many soldiers also suffered mentally. The constant danger, the lack of sleep for days on end, and being continually surrounded by wounded and dying men, had a numbing effect on a soldier's mind, crea-

Recuperating American officers play cards and relax in a peaceful rest home in France in September 1918.

condition known as shell shock. Many victims were sent back to Britain to special hospitals where they received a variety of treatment, from psychotherapy to shock therapy. Wards were filled with the screams of men trapped in their own private nightmares. And the silence of those shuddering in shock was just as terrifying.

As the war went on the level of medical care improved. Doctors and surgeons became used to the new sorts of injuries they faced. Specialists emerged in areas such as plastic surgery, repairing the skin of soldiers who had been badly burned. Because so many people lost arms or legs, the science of prosthetics – or artificial limbs – developed rapidly. And pharmacists found new drugs that could counteract some of the effects of chemical warfare.

Some of the men going into battle hoped to be wounded by a bullet in the arm or the leg so that they would be sent home alive but not permanently damaged. But many of those wounded were disabled for life. After the war it was an all too common sight to see amputees or other crippled veterans begging on the streets to make a living.

Soldiers blinded on the battlefield, often by poison gas, learn to cope with their disability by practicing basic skills, such as basket weaving.

Albert
Peronne
Front Line Mid Sept
Somme
FRANCE

Advance to the HINDENBURG LINE

The Allied victories on the Western Front continued. The German army still fought hard but was headed for defeat.

British troops advance toward the German lines on August 21, 1918. The men are spread out in case of German artillery fire.

<table>
<tr><td rowspan="11">FactFile</td></tr>
</table>

OPPOSING FORCES	German: 66 divisions	Allied: 34 divisions
COMMANDERS	Supreme commander: Ludendorff	Commander in chief: Haig
LOCATION	14-mile front north and east of Albert	
DURATION	August 21 – September 3, 1918	
OUTCOME	Allies advance 25 miles to Hindenburg Line.	
CASUALTIES	German: approx. 115,000	Allied: approx. 89,000

Allied attacks had sent the German forces reeling back on the Marne and at Amiens in July and early August 1918. The Allied leaders were confident and ready to continue attacking. In late August and early September the Allies forced the Germans to give up the last of the territory that they had won in their offensives in the spring. The Germans pulled back to the fortified Hindenburg Line, hoping to halt the Allies there.

Horses and men of a Canadian cavalry unit rest during the Allied advance in early September 1918. The more open conditions in the last months of the war gave cavalry forces a chance to use their superior mobility.

The British advance during the Battle of Amiens had brought their forces into the area where the Battle of the Somme had been fought in 1916. This region was still a devastated wilderness that would hinder the new attacks. Despite this the prospects of success looked good.

Although the German forces outnumbered the British, the British had several advantages. Their morale was much higher. Throughout August German troops had continued to desert the battlefield or surrender to Allied soldiers without much of a fight. The British also had tanks to spearhead their advance. More importantly, their artillery was now much better organized and equipped.

Further south the Germans were also being driven back by the French, who captured the town of Lassigny on August 21. The French Tenth and Third Armies continued to attack the Germans as the British offensive began.

On August 21 the British began to advance to the north and east of the ruined town of Albert. On the first day the British Third Army advanced 3,000 to 4,000 yards, despite fierce German resistance. On the following day the Germans attempted a counterattack, but this was costly and unsuccessful. The British attack was renewed on August 23, with the Third and Fourth Armies driving forward on a front that was now 35 miles wide.

Tanks and artillery in battle

The intense summer heat made conditions extremely difficult for infantry and the gunners. For the tank crews it was unbearable. Many fainted from the heat and fumes inside their tanks.

The tanks themselves were still far from being war winners. After ten days of fighting, some 90 percent of the initial tank force had either broken down or been knocked out. Among the crews casualties from German fire and from exhaustion were also high.

The secret of the British success was not their new weapon but the fact that their attacks were now far better coordinated. The infantry and artillery worked together very efficiently, helped by the tanks if they were available.

Continuing the advance

On August 26 the battle front widened, as the British First Army, which included Canadian troops, attacked to the north, beyond the town of Arras. Far to the south the French Tenth Army added support by crossing the important Aisne River.

Australian and Canadian troops showed special bravery in the attacks. The Australians captured strong German positions on Mont St. Quentin on August 31. To the north the Canadians took equally well-defended positions between Drocourt and Quéant on September 2.

On September 3 these continuing defeats brought a general German retreat to the Hindenburg Line, the defensive positions which had been the starting point for their offensive of March 1918. Virtually all their gains from the hard fighting earlier in the year had now been given up.

By the middle of September, however, the British advance had ground to a halt. Field Marshal Haig had committed all the available reserves and was unable to exploit the victory further for the moment. The British, French, Canadian, and Australian troops had sustained considerable casualties. The German army was on the retreat, and its morale was crumbling, but it remained a formidable opponent.

A German transport driver lies dead with his horses after being hit by Allied artillery fire during the fighting in September 1918.

Mortars

Mortars are short-barreled artillery weapons that throw projectiles up in a high arc, dropping them on top of and behind enemy defenses. The main ammunition employed in modern times has been high explosive shells.

Although mortars were first used in the 16th century, the necessary technology developed very slowly before World War I. Before the war, however, the Germans had developed various types of mortar as infantry support weapons. They became the model for those used by all armies in the war.

Mortars played an important role in trench warfare, including the Allied offensives of 1918, because of their effectiveness against fortified defensive positions. They had much shorter ranges than traditional artillery guns but could be manhandled into trenches and used there, which artillery guns could not.

Some mortars could fire very large shells that could smash a section of enemy trench, but these types were heavier and more difficult to get into position. The British developed a lighter and more maneuverable type known as the Stokes mortar. Mortars basically similar to this are still used by modern armies.

A British Stokes mortar team in action on the Balkan Front.

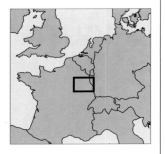

ST. MIHIEL

The Battle of St. Mihiel was a clear-cut victory won by American troops. It was the first battle in the war in which an independent American force fought under U.S. command.

Dug-in for cover in the flat landscape, men of the U.S. 42nd Division prepare to continue their advance in the St. Mihiel salient on September 15, 1918.

FactFile

OPPOSING FORCES	German: 75,000	American: 216,000
		French: 50,000
COMMANDERS	Fuchs	Pershing
LOCATION	Southwest of Verdun and northeast of Nancy	
DURATION	September 12 – 13, 1918	
OUTCOME	Allies clear German-occupied St. Mihiel salient.	
CASUALTIES	German: 15,000 taken prisoner	American: 7,000

The battle of St. Mihiel was the first time that the troops of the American Expeditionary Force or AEF fought as a separate fighting unit under the command of their own generals. When American troops had fought earlier in the year it was as part of British or French armies. But General Pershing, commander of the AEF, was determined that the American troops should form their own independent force.

EYEWITNESS

Douglas MacArthur, a brigade commander during the St. Mihiel offensive, left a vivid account of his impressions after liberating a French town:

66 In Essey I saw a sight I shall never forget. Our advance had been so rapid the Germans had evacuated in a panic. There was a German officer's horse saddled and equipped standing in a barn, a battery of guns complete in every detail, and the entire instrumentation and music of a regimental band. The town was still occupied by civilians, mostly old men, women, and children.... They did not know that United States soldiers were in the war.... They were started at once to the rear. Men, women, and children plodded along in mud up to their knees carrying what few household effects they could. It was one of the most forlorn sights I have ever seen. 99

Below: The main American advances which cleared the St. Mihiel salient.

Bottom: An American machine gunner takes aim on the enemy from a well-camouflaged firing position.

In mid-August 1918 Pershing got his way and the U.S. First Army became operational. The target for their first battle was a vulnerable salient, or bulge, in the German lines at St. Mihiel, southeast of Verdun.

General Ludendorff knew that the German forces at St. Mihiel were in danger and planned to retreat. But the German High Command was still taken by surprise when the attack began on September 12. They had fallen for a trick by American counterintelligence and were therefore expecting an offensive further south,

The attack force included some 260 tanks which played a key role in the American advance. Lieutenant-Colonel George S. Patton, a tank commander, told his men on the day before the attack: "American tanks do not surrender so long as one tank is able to go forward.... Its presence will save the lives of hundreds of infantry and kill many Germans."

On September 12, 216,000 American troops advanced, backed by another 50,000 French soldiers. As well as the tanks and 3,000 guns, they also had 1,500 aircraft in support. They caught the Germans in the

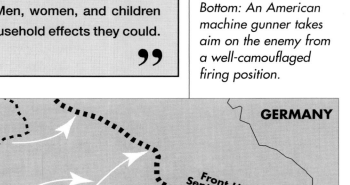

FRANCE   GERMANY

Front Line September 16

Vigneulles

St Mihiel

Front Line September 12

Far right: An American ammunition wagon stuck in the road holds up a whole column of supply vehicles. The poor quality of the roads near St. Mihiel made such traffic jams a common occurrence.

men of the future

George S. Patton

Born in 1885 in California, George Patton was descended from an old Virginia family. He graduated from West Point in 1909 and became an aide to General Pershing in 1916.

Patton was chosen to go to France with Pershing in 1917. It was there that Patton developed his lifelong belief in the value of tanks in military combat. Patton commanded a tank brigade in the St. Mihiel battle and was wounded in the subsequent Meuse-Argonne offensive.

In World War II Patton fought with the U.S. forces in their campaign in North Africa during 1942 and then led the U.S. Seventh Army in the invasion of Sicily in 1943. After D-Day in 1944 Patton commanded the U.S. Third Army during the liberation of France. His armies were famous for their rapid attacks, led by tank forces. His forces crossed the Rhine River in March 1945 and advanced into the heart of Germany.

Patton had a difficult personality. He could be obstinate and rude, and was always controversial. However, he was also one of the most successful American generals ever. He was killed in an accident in 1945, after the end of World War II

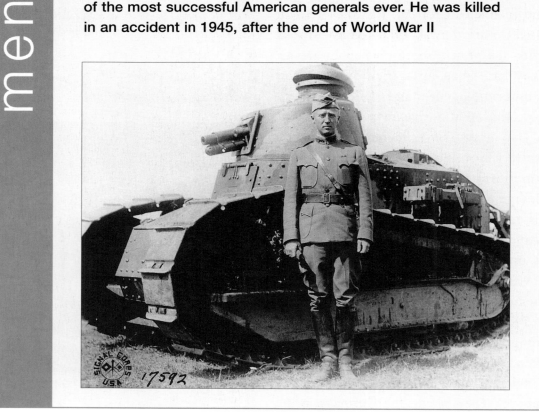

Right: Colonel Patton poses in front of a Renault light tank at a training camp in France in 1918.

THE COMMANDERS

**Hunter Liggett
1857–1935
American general**
Hunter Liggett was born in Reading, Pennsylvania. He joined the U.S. Army and served on the western frontier and in the Spanish-American War and Philippine insurrection.

By the time of the U.S. entry into World War I he had established a reputation as the "soundest reasoner and strongest realist in the American army."

He commanded the I Corps from the start of 1918 and played a major part in the St. Mihiel battle. He was then promoted and achieved further success as commander of the First Army during the Meuse-Argonne Offensive, in which Allied forces pierced the Hindenburg Line.

alternatives

What if the Americans had continued their attack at St. Mihiel? Douglas MacArthur, who served in the battle, believed that they could have captured the German-held city of Metz, opening a way into southern Germany. He was probably wrong. The American victory at St. Mihiel had only driven the Germans from a salient they had already decided to abandon. The Allied commanders had decided to concentrate elsewhere on the Western Front. MacArthur overestimated the quality of his own troops, who had run short of supplies at St. Mihiel, and underestimated the German will to fight on.

middle of the withdrawal that Ludendorff had ordered. The 75,000 German troops were battle-weary. They could not match the freshness and determination of the numerically superior American troops.

Within 48 hours the Americans had captured some 13,000 prisoners and taken 200 German guns. At midday on September 13 it was French troops who actually entered the town of St. Mihiel. But it was the American attacks on the flanks which had won the victory.

The success at St. Mihiel was more significant in terms of prestige than in terms of the outcome of the war. The German decision to withdraw had been made before the American attack and, in a sense, the attack only hastened this process. However, it did prove that American troops, under American leadership, could defeat the German army in battle.

WHERE TO FIND...

AEF: 5:29
Pershing: 5:28
Ludendorff: 7:34
Meuse-Argonne Offensive: 7:88

The UNITED STATES AT WAR

Reports from France confirmed the American people's pride in their army. Americans united in their support for the war.

A train carrying tobacco to be shipped to the men in France is decorated with patriotic advertising slogans.

By the fall of 1918 the American people were generally united in their support for the war. Government propaganda campaigns and an upsurge in patriotic fervor had contributed to a mood of national unity. Members of groups suspected of being hostile to the war, such as German-Americans, tried to show that their primary loyalty was to the United States, and that charges that they favored the Central Powers were untrue. Opponents of the conflict, such as pacifists and socialists, were disregarded or forced to keep silent.

Most Americans wanted the war to end with a clear victory rather than a compromise peace. The American army's success in the summer battles gave people confi-

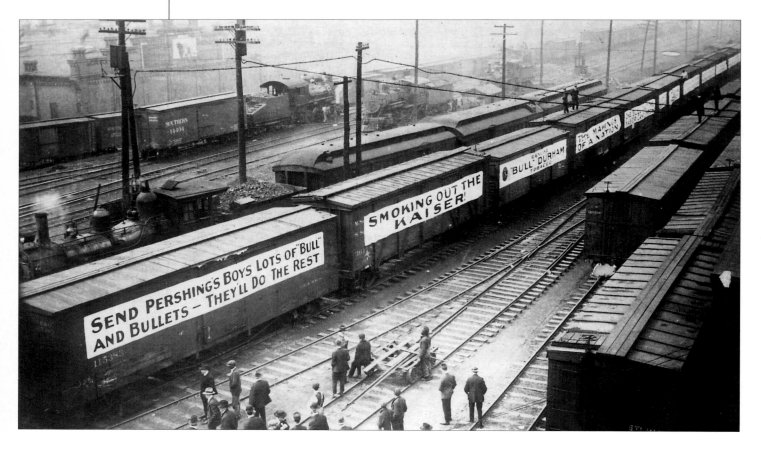

HOUSEWIVES FOR LIBERTY! HELP WAGE OUR BATTLES In the Kitchen.

Housewives in Philadelphia parade to convince others not to waste food so that the Allied nations do not go hungry. U.S. war propaganda stressed that everyone at home had a part to play in the war effort.

dence that this victory could be achieved quickly. This confidence was accompanied by quiet satisfaction, rather than jubilation, on the home front. People were relieved that the army's training seemed to have paid dividends on the battlefield.

Ordinary Americans felt that the successes at Belleau Wood and St. Mihiel contradicted German charges that the American army was no match for their own. *The New York Times* summed up the feelings of the bulk of the population: "There is a thrill for the American people in the news of their First Army in battle.... They have longed to see their own Army in action, having faith in its invincibility, and desiring a demonstration of its soldierly qualities, not only to impress our brave Allies, but to show the Germans how Americans, whom they have disparaged and affected to despise, can fight for a just cause. The glorious day has come at last."

President Wilson was pleased, too. He sent a telegram congratulating Pershing on the army's success. "The boys have done what we expected of them," the president wrote, "and done it in the way we most admire. We are deeply proud of them and their Chief."

The Americans had also won the respect of their allies. A leading British newspaper, *The Times*, described the U.S. Army's success at St. Mihiel in glowing terms: "We rejoice that the first great enterprise undertaken by the United States' forces on the Western Front has had such swift and dramatic results. The place and time alike were happily chosen, and the Germans have had a salutary example of the power of the American sword."

WHERE TO FIND...

Peace or War for the United States: 4:110

The U.S. Enters the War: 5:26

Belleau Wood: 7:54

St. Mihiel: 7:76

Pershing: 5:28

Black Americans in

Right: A black infantry unit in the trenches in France.

Below: A proud father displays 11 stars to show that he has that number of close relatives serving in the armed forces. Families with sons, husbands, or fathers in the army would display stars in the windows of their homes to signal their contribution to the war effort.

During World War I 400,000 black men and women served in the United States' armed forces. Many of them hoped that by offering their lives for their country, they would achieve a greater measure of racial equality in the United States. Their hopes were not to be fulfilled.

Blacks were discriminated against throughout the armed forces. A disproportionate number of black men were drafted into the military. During the war 13 percent of U.S. Army personnel were black, even though African-Americans made up only 10 per

the Army

EYEWITNESS

Charles Houston, who served as a Lieutenant in the 92nd Division of the AEF in France, and later became Dean of the Howard University Law School, recalled that he, and other black officers, were treated disrespectfully by white American soldiers:

66 The hate and scorn heaped upon us as Negro officers by Americans at Camp Mencou and Vannes in France, convinced me there was no sense of dying in a world ruled by them.... They made us eat on benches in order to maintain segregation and they destroyed our prestige in front of French officers. 99

cent of the American population at that time.

The army maintained a rigid color line. Blacks and whites were segregated into separate regiments. Many blacks hoped to serve as combat troops. Most black troops, however, were never allowed to fight for their country in battle. Almost all black troops were assigned to work behind the lines as laborers. The few black units that did serve in battle, such as the 92nd (Colored) Regiment, fought well.

White soldiers often refused to salute black officers. Very few blacks, however well qualified, were ever allowed to rise above the comparatively junior rank of captain. Only one percent of U.S. Army officers were black.

White officers, particularly from the segregationist South, tried to prevent black soldiers from associating with French people, whose attitudes toward race were more relaxed than those of most American whites. They feared that the blacks would be encouraged to rebel against segregation when they returned to the United States.

The great contribution of blacks to the war effort was not acknowledged by whites. In response many black Americans came to believe that, for them, the war had been fought in vain.

Black soldiers prepare for work with an engineer unit in France. Wartime photographs such as this tended to reinforce racial stereotypes, like black men happily engaged in laboring work.

Salonika:
VARDAR OFFENSIVE

With their full-scale attack on the Salonika front, the Allies aimed not only to crush Bulgaria for good but to weaken the resolve of the entire Central Powers to fight on.

Bulgarian infantry machine-gun teams in the hilly terrain near Monastir.

FactFile

OPPOSING FORCE	Bulgarian: 15 divisions	Allied: 28 divisions
COMMANDERS	Crown Prince Boris	General Louis Franchet d'Esperey
LOCATION	Macedonia, on the Serb–Greek border	
DURATION	September 14 – 30, 1918 (some fighting continued until the armistice on November 4)	
OUTCOME	The Allies knock Bulgaria out of the war.	
CASUALTIES	Bulgarian: approx. 80,000; plus approx. 77,000 taken prisoner	Allied: approx. 16,000

In September 1918 the Allies launched a final, massive assault against Bulgarian and German troops on the border between Greece and Serbia. Their advance along the valley of the Vardar River, the main communication route between northern Greece and central Europe, would force the Bulgarians back, and lead ultimately to their surrender.

On September 14 French General Franchet d'Esperey's Allied troops opened their attack with an artillery bombard-

French troops march through the town of Monastir after it had fallen to the Allied advance.

ment. It destroyed much of the enemy's barbed wire but left machine-gun nests and artillery positions intact. Despite this, the Serbian and French troops managed to advance. The next day they pushed across the frontier between Greece and Serbia.

Their progress was not easy. Although the Allies had more men and artillery, the mountainous terrain favored the defenders. The Bulgarians were secured in fortified positions. But the French found a way to dislodge them: They used flamethrowers for the first time in the war.

One British newspaper admired the achievement of their French and Serb allies: "This success has been won in the face of immense difficulties. The Bulgarian lines were drawn in a region among mountains from 4,000 feet to 5,000 feet high, which have been fortified by the enemy for two and a half years."

On September 16 mutiny broke out among the demoralized Bulgarian forces, who refused to fight on. The German commander on the Salonika front, General von

Scholtz, realized that the mutiny could not be put down and ordered a limited retreat. Meanwhile, the Allied advance continued.

On September 18 British and Greek troops attacked the Bulgarians at Lake Dorian, east of the Vardar. At first they made slow progress against machine-gun fire. But by September 20 they had occupied the town of Dorian. On the same day the Bulgarian army, facing defeat and collapsing from within, retreated. Five days later the French liberated the capital of Serbian Macedonia, Skopje.

The crushing defeat of the army led to civil unrest in Bulgaria itself. On September 23 revolutionary councils, known as soviets, were established in several Bulgarian towns. Within a week the government asked the Allies for an armistice. By mid-October Allied troops occupied the Bulgarian capital, Sofia.

The Allies had won a stunning victory. But the fighting in Serbia was not over yet; it would continue until the Allies could defeat the Austrians.

WHERE TO FIND...

Franchet d'Esperey: 7:46

Flamethrowers: 7:48

Salonika: 3:106; **4:**86; **5:**48

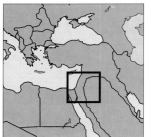

The MEGIDDO OFFENSIVE

With their superior air power and fast cavalry, the Allies were able to gain a decisive victory in the Middle East, driving the Turks north toward Damascus.

In September 1918 the British resumed their offensive against the Turks in Palestine. Their capture of Jerusalem in 1917 had brought the Allied advance to a halt. But in 1918 they would push Turkey out of the war for good.

An instant success

Just before the British launched their assault on September 19, they heavily bombarded the Turkish positions with artillery. Then they attacked along the Mediterranean coastal plain. British commander General Edmund Allenby's forces then swung inland, through hilly, barren Palestine toward the Jordan River. The offensive had barely begun and already the British infantry had broken through Turkish lines. The cavalry was rapidly advancing along the coastal plain.

As well as fast cavalry, air power was crucial to the Allies' success. On September 20 British and Australian aircraft bombed Turkish and German telephone exchanges and telegraph offices. This attack cut off contact between the German overall commander of the Turkish forces, General Liman von Sanders, and his junior officers. The Allies also destroyed the main German airfield. From now on they could bomb roads, railroads, and enemy troops without fear of counterattack.

Turkish troops, still in their trenches, are taken prisoner by Allied soldiers on April 29, 1918.

Allied cavalry charge into a Palestinian town on their rapid advance toward Jerusalem.

The Allied attack quickly turned into a decisive victory. Turkish troops began to desert. Von Sanders ordered them to make a stand near Megiddo, now in Israel. The Allies found little resistance there: The only shots fired against them came from nine German riflemen. On September 21 British cavalrymen reached the town of Nazareth. The Allies had advanced 40 miles in just one day.

FactFile			
OPPOSING FORCES (Sept. 19)	Turkish: 25,000 infantry 3,000 cavalry	British: 56,000 infantry 11,000 cavalry Arab: at least 3,000	
COMMANDERS	Turkish: von Sanders	British: Allenby	
LOCATION	Northern coastal plain of Palestine		
DURATION	Sept. 19 – 26, 1918		
OUTCOME	Allied victory ultimately forces the Turks out of the war.		
CASUALTIES (Total offensive)	Turkish: 45,000 taken prisoner	British: approx. 5,500	

Crushing the Turks

The Turks fled. They retreated through hills and narrow valleys toward the Jordan River. The retreat soon became a massacre. For three days the British and Australians bombed and machine-gunned the Turks in the valley of the Wadi Fara. Allied aircraft dropped 19 tons of bombs and fired 119,000 machine-gun rounds at the targets. Hundreds of Turks were killed.

On September 23 the British continued their advance along the coast. The cavalry captured the ancient city of Haifa. The Allies then struck their final blow, crossing the Jordan to capture the city of Amman, an important railroad junction.

The Allies had triumphed, capturing some 45,000 Turkish and German prisoners in a week. Allenby's forces continued to crush the Turks as they retreated north toward Damascus. The Turks would not recover from their defeat: In a month's time, on October 30, 1918, they would request an armistice. Their war was over, and German defeat was not far behind.

WHERE TO FIND...

Capture of Jerusalem: 5:108
Allenby: 5:110
Defeat of the German Army: 7:94

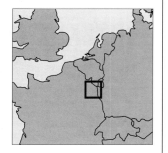

The Meuse-Argonne OFFENSIVE

The U.S. Army pushed the Germans back despite difficult terrain, fierce resistance, and its own inexperience.

American artillerymen in action with a massive long-range gun. Special railroads often had to be laid to bring such guns into action at the front.

FactFile

OPPOSING FORCES	German: 40 divisions	Allied: approx. 700,000
COMMANDERS	von der Marwitz, Einem	American: Pershing French: Gouraud
LOCATION	Northeast France	
DURATION	September 26 – November 11, 1918	
OUTCOME	Allied victory and the end of the war.	
CASUALTIES	German: 100,000; plus 26,000 taken prisoner	American: 117,000 French: not known

American troops had fought – and fought well – at Belleau Wood. But the doughboys, as the American troops were called, still had to prove themselves in a large, sustained operation. The chance would come in the drive through the forests of the Argonne and toward the Meuse River. It was not only the army that was on trial. Its commander, General Pershing, had insisted on keeping his armies separate from those of the

Western Front

Left: American infantry resting after capturing a German trench. A sentry keeps watch in case of a German counterattack.

Below: Map showing the American advance during the Meuse-Argonne offensive.

Allies. Now the wisdom of his policy would be tested.

Although Pershing kept command of the U.S. troops, the Meuse-Argonne attack was part of a coordinated offensive along the whole Western Front. The Allies aimed to break through the Hindenburg Line of German defenses. The Americans lay on the right flank of the advance. If they failed, the French forces to the west would be in danger. The plan was for the French and Americans to trap the German defenders in a pincer movement and then to advance 30 miles and capture the towns of Mézières and Sedan.

On the morning of September 26 a massive artillery bombardment signaled the

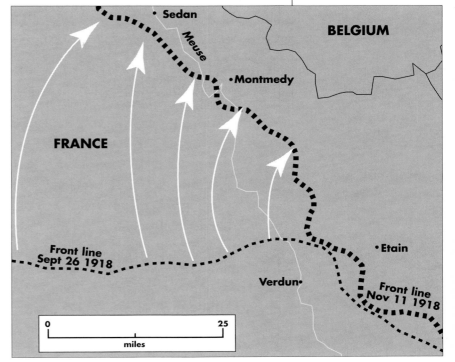

BELGIUM

FRANCE

• Sedan

Meuse

• Montmedy

• Etain

Front line
Sept 26 1918

Verdun•

Front line
Nov 11 1918

0   25
miles

Horse-drawn vehicles and trucks amid the congestion behind American lines. It rained on virtually every day of the Meuse-Argonne battle. Muddy roads made the transportation problems even worse.

Allied attack. On the American part of the front Pershing sent 700 tanks to lead the assault. Behind them came the U.S. First Army now 15 divisions strong. The first day of the offensive was successful. The Allies advanced three miles and took 23,000 Germans prisoner.

Such a pace proved hard to sustain. The German positions were heavily fortified, and their troops fought hard. Among the steep, tree-covered slopes and ridges of the Argonne Forest the U.S. troops made slow progress against the dug-in defenders. To the east other American units attacked over less difficult ground. The Germans, however, had more elaborate defenses here. And when they retreated, they devastated everything they left behind that might be useful to the attackers – a tactic called "scorched earth." Both attackers and defenders sustained heavy casualties.

Four days into the attack the American offensive ground to a halt.

The attack was relaunched on October 4. Again progress was slow. It was not until October 10 that the First Army finally succeeded in pushing the Germans out of the Argonne Forest.

Chaos behind the lines

The Americans' slow progress upset some of the Allies. They blamed Pershing and wanted him to be relieved of his command. Not only were his troops demoralized; the army itself was disorganized. There were problems with supplies and transportation. Huge traffic jams clogged the roads behind the front. Generals did not have supplies to launch attacks. The soldiers in the front line had no food or ammunition. Pershing himself recorded that his men were "disorganized, and apparently disheartened."

In some ways the problems were inevitable given the numbers of U.S. troops. Inexperienced American staff officers were struggling to cope with supply and administrative problems for their new and rapidly growing armies. By October there were so many American troops in France that a U.S. Second Army was formed.

On November 1 the First Army finally made a breakthrough. Bolstered by reinforcements, the Americans began their advance. It was preceded by an artillery bombardment and heavy bombing of the German lines by aircraft. The Germans broke and retreated northward. By November 6 the Americans had reached the outskirts of their original target – the town of Sedan.

Fighting continued until the end of the war on November 11. The doughboys and Pershing had proved themselves, but at a price. The campaign in the Meuse-Argonne saw 117,000 American casualties. No other U.S. offensive had been so costly.

WAR PROFILES

Alvin C. York
1887-1964
War hero

Alvin Cullum York was born in Pall Mall, Tennessee. At first he thought of refusing to join the army because his Christian faith taught him that killing was wrong.

During the Meuse-Argonne offensive, on October 8, 1918, York led a squad of men against German positions. He himself killed 25 of the enemy with rifle shots and took 132 prisoner. The exploit made this modest man the greatest American hero of the war. He was awarded the Medal of Honor. A film of his life was later made starring Gary Cooper.

EYEWITNESS

Amos N. Wilder, an American soldier who took part in the Meuse-Argonne offensive, kept a diary of his experiences. The entry for November 5 indicates that German resistance was determined, and that supply problems hindered the American advance.

66 The Germans were resisting. Instead of a mere march, the operation of the 3rd became an attack. Headquarters moved to Bayonville – and on the 4th to Fosse – the infantry being at Beaumont and the river on the 5th. The weather is so bad that the ammunition cannot come up. Last night clear – and the Boche were bombing all about these villages – few here if any – but an allied 9" [gun] in the neighborhood kept us awake – us and the window frames. 99

Sergeant York photographed on the hillside on which he won his Medal of Honor.

WHERE TO FIND...

Congressional
ELECTIONS

In 1918 the Democrats lost control of the Congress. Republicans would govern the U.S. throughout the 1920s.

President Wilson watches a baseball tournament with his wife (right) and mother-in-law (left).

During the war Democratic President Woodrow Wilson tried to convince the American people that he was a truly national leader who was above party politics. Wilson told Americans that the war set aside the usual concerns of party politics. He claimed that as long as the war went on, "politics is adjourned." But Wilson's actions contrasted with his words.

Wilson refused to work with leading Republicans, such as ex-President Theodore Roosevelt and Senator Henry Cabot Lodge. Some members of his own administration and many Democrats in Congress also thought he made too many decisions without consultation.

The Congressional elections of November 1918 gave the Republicans a chance to cut Wilson down to size. Although they had not controlled Congress since 1910, they believed they could win a majority of seats in 1918. Wilson was acting in a high-handed fashion. He turned down moderate Republicans who offered to work with him. Then he upset his own party by trying to prevent Democratic congressmen who had voted against the war from running for office on the party's electoral ticket.

When Americans went to the polls, Wilson urged them to elect Democrats. He said that this was not for party political reasons but "for the sake of the nation itself."

An artist and his model at work producing a famous U.S. Marine recruiting poster. The model is shown taking off his jacket and getting ready to fight.

Many people found his claim hard to believe. His appeal on behalf of the Democrats spoiled his image as an impartial national leader.

In the 1918 elections the Republicans won control of both the Senate and the House of Representatives. Many people believed the defeat was caused by Wilson's personal unpopularity.

Republican control of Congress would make life difficult for Wilson. In 1919, for example, the Senate refused to support the peace treaty he negotiated. This decision would have far-reaching consequences.

WHERE TO FIND...

Reelection of Wilson: 4:108

Paris Peace Conference: 8:28

Peace Treaties: 8:36

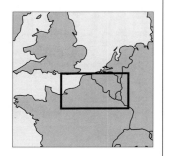

The Defeat of the
GERMAN ARMY

Beaten in battle after battle and pushed back to their own borders by a coordinated Allied offensive, the German generals eventually realized the war must end.

A British general makes a speech to his men by the banks of the St. Quentin Canal on September 29, 1918. He is congratulating his troops for having successfully crossed the canal in their attack the day before.

FactFile

OPPOSING FORCES	German: 183.5 infantry divisions; 4 cavalry divisions	Allied (Nov): 207 infantry divisions; 9 cavalry divisions
COMMANDERS	Supreme commander: Ludendorff	Supreme commander: Foch
LOCATION	From Ypres in the north to Argonne in the south	
DURATION	September 27 – November 11, 1918	
OUTCOME	Allies advance and Germany signs an armistice.	
CASUALTIES	German: Unknown	Allied: Unknown

The Allied successes in August and September 1918 had shaken the entire German army. From late September to the end of the war in November the Allies inflicted yet more defeats on the Germans. The Allies drove forward relentlessly. The most important attacks were made by the British, often spearheaded by Canadian and Australian troops.

Allied commander Marshal Foch planned four attacks. American troops

politics

Ludendorff resigns

The success of the Allied offensive at Amiens in August 1918 shocked Germany's military dictatorship. General Ludendorff, who effectively ran the country, lost his nerve and wanted an armistice, but he was not prepared to contemplate peace on unfavorable terms. Some other army commanders had concluded by mid-August that defeat was inevitable. Crown Prince Rupprecht of Bavaria, the commander of the German army in Flanders, wrote on August 15: "Our military situation has deteriorated so rapidly that I no longer believe we can hold out over the winter." By the end of September 1918, with Allied offensives driving the Germans back along the whole Western Front, Ludendorff called for an immediate end to the war.

As the Allied offensive slowed in mid-October, Ludendorff changed his mind. He now said that Germany should fight on and attack again in 1919. Eventually Ludendorff went too far. On October 24 he issued an order for German troops to "fight to the finish." The Kaiser was furious that Ludendorff had issued such an order without consulting him. On October 25 Ludendorff resigned. He was replaced by General Gröner, who took a more realistic view of the situation and realized that Germany must end the war.

A map shows the main thrusts of the Allied advances on the Western Front in the last three months of the war.

would move through the Meuse-Argonne; the French would advance in Champagne. Meanwhile the British would strike between Cambrai and St. Quentin, and around Ypres.

The Allies faced two main problems. First, the Germans had now fallen back to the formidable Hindenburg Line. This defensive system had been carefully fortified more than a year before and had been the base from which they had begun their advances in the spring. Second, as the Allies advanced, they had to cross the wastelands of former battles, which now

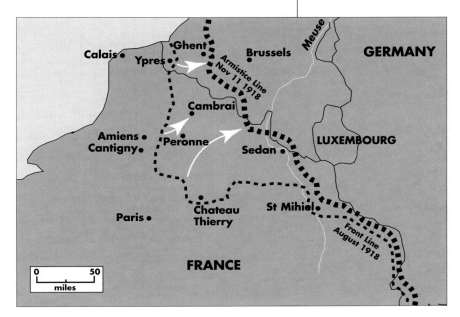

the armies

Anzacs in France

Anzacs (Australian and New Zealand) troops arrived on the Western Front in 1916 and saw action during the First Battle of the Somme. In 1917 the Australians and New Zealanders were involved in the fighting at Arras, Messines, and Ypres. During that year they sustained 50,000 casualties. They led the Allied attack during the Amiens offensive of August 1918 and, together with the Canadian forces, spearheaded the final British advances that ended the war. The Australians showed particular courage during the operation to capture the heavily fortified German positions at Mont St. Quentin on August 31 and September 1. In that one action eight Australian soldiers won the Victoria Cross, the highest award in the British empire for bravery.

The Anzacs had a talented leader, General Sir John Monash. He carefully coordinated tanks and artillery with his infantry attacks to keep casualties as low as possible and ensure success. Between August 8 and October 5 the Australians captured 116 towns and villages, and advanced almost 40 miles. During that time they lost 3,566 men.

The Anzacs disliked drill and conventional army discipline, which made them unpopular with some British officers. But their units were also recognized as some of the toughest and most effective fighters on the Allied side.

lay just behind the Allied front. They had to move all their supplies forward over empty, muddy, and cratered ground, building roads and railroad lines as they went.

The British and French attacks started on September 27, the day after the American advance in the Meuse-Argonne. Because of problems caused by the terrain, the offensive took the form of a series of smaller advances, which halted after a few days to reorganize. The Allied generals had been criticized earlier in the war for con-tinuing attacks after they had lost momentum and thereby causing unnecessary casualties. They did not make this mistake now.

Rapid progress

The British attack between Cambrai and St. Quentin moved quickly, taking many prisoners. On September 28 a new British attack drove east from Ypres. The Germans could not stop the advance.

Early in October the Allies successfully overran a 30-mile-long section of the

alternatives

What if the Germans had continued fighting in November 1918? Many German troops felt betrayed by the Armistice. They blamed Germany's defeat on revolutionaries and civilian politicians. The soldiers believed that they had not been beaten, but had been "stabbed in the back." Many right-wingers refused to accept the German republic created in 1919. Later they supported Adolf Hitler, who attacked the "November criminals" of 1918.

But Germany's High Command knew that the army had been defeated. With poor supplies of food and ammunition, and with troops weary of battle, they could not go on fighting. If they had, Germany's defeat would have been greater than it actually was. Germany would have been invaded and occupied; the peace settlement would have been harsher. But the soldiers would not have been able to claim that they had been betrayed by politicians. The chances for creating a stable democracy in Germany after the war might have been greater.

Hindenburg Line. The fall of the line – once thought virtually impregnable – stunned German commander General Erich Ludendorff. He argued that Germany should request an immediate armistice. Still, the advance went on. The British and French began new offensives. Once more the weary Germans retreated.

Despite the Allies' success, late October saw German resistance stiffen again. Now Ludendorff spoke of being able to prevent an Allied victory before winter. British Field Marshal Sir Douglas Haig agreed. He suggested that the war might drag on into 1919. Both men were mistaken.

On November 8 the Allies crossed another barrier on the way to Germany – the Scheldt River. By the time the Armistice halted fighting on November 11, they had also captured Ghent and Mons. Such victories, combined with the growing strength of the U.S. forces in France, made the defeat of the German army complete.

1918
SEPTEMBER-NOVEMBER

Western Front

A French trench mortar crew goes into action in 1918.

WHERE TO FIND...

Foch: **7:**33

Meuse-Argonne
  Offensive: **7:**88

Haig: **4:**70

Armistice: **7:**112

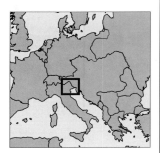

AUSTRIA-
HUNGARY

Trento
Piave
Vittorio
Veneto
Front Line
October 1918
Venice
ITALY
ADRIATIC
SEA

The Battle of
VITTORIO VENETO

The last battle on the Italian front would bring revenge for the Allied attackers and humiliating surrender for the Austro-Hungarian forces.

British troops eagerly fill their water bottles from a hillside spring in Italy. British troops fought on the Italian front during 1917 and 1918.

OPPOSING FORCES	Austrian: 54.5 infantry divisions; 6 dismounted cavalry divisions	Allied: 57 infantry divisions; 4 cavalry divisions
COMMANDERS	von Straussenburg	Diaz
LOCATION	Northeast Italy	
DURATION	October 23 – November 4, 1918	
OUTCOME	Italian victory forces Austrians to make peace.	
CASUALTIES	Austrian: approx. 30,000	Allied: approx. 41,000

In October 1918 the Allies launched what would prove a final offensive against the Austrians in northeast Italy. During the summer Italian chief of staff General Diaz had limited himself to local operations. But now that the Germans were falling back on the Western Front, he felt confident enough to take on the Austrians without fear of German intervention. The attack would have a dramatic result – the collapse of the Austrian army.

There were two main thrusts to the offensive. Diaz aimed to attack the Austrians in the mountains of Trentino and to launch another assault across the Piave River toward the town of Vittorio Veneto. The opposing sides had fought over the same land many times before.

A superior force

The Allied force assembled for the attack was overwhelmingly Italian, though it included a few British and French divisions, as well as smaller numbers of American and Czech troops. The army they faced was smaller, had less artillery, and was weakened by three years of tough mountain fighting.

On October 23 Diaz launched his assault in the region of Mount Grappa in Trentino. It was difficult to advance. The going was tough in the mountainous terrain, and the Austrians, in strong positions, fought with great determination. But the Austrians' shortage of men told against them. To reinforce their overstretched defenders, they had to move men from the lower Piave Valley. That opened the way for the Allies to advance on the Adriatic coastal plain. On October 27 British and Italian troops managed to cross the Piave. The Austrians retreated, and 7,000 of their men were taken prisoner.

Within three days the Allies had advanced 15 miles. Many of the retreating

American soldiers on the Piave front hurl a shower of hand grenades toward the Austrian trenches, September 16, 1918.

Prisoners of war

During 1918, as the Central Powers came close to defeat, the numbers of prisoners captured were higher than ever.

In 1907 The Hague Rules had set guidelines for the treatment of prisoners of war, or POWs. They were not to be ill-treated or made to work too hard; they were to have adequate food, clothing, and accommodation, and be allowed to receive parcels from home. For some men, becoming a prisoner was an attractive alternative to facing death in the trenches.

In fact, the treatment of POWs varied enormously. The guidelines were not always strictly observed, and men on all sides reported stories of ill-treatment. One British soldier, captured by the Germans, recorded in his diary: "Interpreter asked if anyone wanted to go sick and one man unwisely said he did. The officer came and looked at him, and then gave him a punch in the face which knocked him down." Another British officer recalled being offered cigarettes and champagne by a German officer when he was first captured. Soon after, he found himself in a bare, bitterly cold, and stinking cell.

The quality of prisoners' food also varied. Prisoners were meant to receive rations similar to those of the civilian population. But Allied POWs in Germany saw their rations get smaller during the war, as the Germans struggled against food shortages. Relief organizations, such as the Red Cross, supplied prisoners with food parcels. Soldiers lucky enough to receive parcels from home often shared them with their friends.

Some prisoners were forced to work very hard. British, French, and Russian prisoners were sometimes employed in German coal mines. German POWs in Britain usually worked in the fields, helping to bring in the harvest.

German prisoners scowl through the barbed wire of a French prison camp.

Left: Italian troops guard Austrian prisoners in November 1918.

Far Left: A British army "No Blame" letter sent to a former prisoner of war. British officers who had been prisoners had to give a formal explanation of how they had been captured. They could face trial if this explanation was unsatisfactory.

Austrian troops had had enough. They were weary and weak. Back home political tensions had begun to destroy the Austro-Hungarian empire from within. With nothing clear to fight for, the army also began to collapse. Mutinies broke out among the exhausted men.

Austria-Hungary makes peace

On October 28 Emperor Karl of Austria asked the Allies for an armistice: It went into effect on November 4. Meanwhile, the Italians had seized the town of Vittorio Veneto, and the British and French captured the mountain town of Trento.

The Allies had taken 300,000 prisoners in the campaign. The Italians had gained revenge for their humiliating defeat by the Austrians at Caporetto in 1917. And for Austria the war was over.

WAR OFFICE,

subject should be addressed to—
The Secretary,
War Office,
London, S.W.1.

LONDON, S.W.1.

and the above number quoted.

June, 1919.

171914/5 A.G.3(P.W.)

The Secretary of the War Office presents his compliments

to ___2nd Lieutenant W. A. Williams,

___Royal Field Artillery.___

and begs to state that he is commanded by the Army Council to inform him that his statement regarding the circumstances of his capture by the enemy having been investigated, the Council considers that no blame attaches to him in the matter.

The investigation was carried out by a Standing Committee of Enquiry composed as follows :—

Major-General L. A. E. PRICE-DAVIES, V.C., C.M.G., D.S.O.

Brigadier-General C. R. J. GRIFFITH, C.B., C.M.G., D.S.O.

Brevet-Lieut.-Col. E. L. CHALLENOR, C.B., C.M.G., D.S.O.

Unrest in
ITALY

As the effects of war made life at home increasingly difficult, the Italian people turned away from their inept rulers.

Italian soldiers firing their rifles in an anti-aircraft exercise. German and Austrian aircraft made a few attacks on Italian towns.

Italy, like the United States, had entered the war as a divided nation. Both countries were split between those who were in favor of war and those who were against it. In the United States these divisions had broken down by 1918, as Americans united in support of the war effort. In Italy the people remained divided. Indeed, the war increased the underlying tensions in Italian society.

Different groups in Italy despised the country's political system. Although it was liberal and possessed a parliament, many did not believe the government was democratic. Nationalists wanted a right-wing dictatorship to replace it. Socialists, on the other hand, felt that they lived in a class-based system which kept workers and peasants powerless.

The war did nothing to heal this division. Many Italians felt that politicians had allowed their country to be dragged into the war for feeble reasons. Army commanders, meanwhile, insisted that the politicians should stay out of military decision-making. Such an arrangement allowed the army to take the credit for any victories it won, while blaming any defeats on the politicians who took Italy into the war in the first place. As public dissatisfaction with politicians grew, nationalists hoped that Italians would rise up against a corrupt political system. And socialists, who opposed the war, dreamed that it would be followed by revolution.

Military morale was dangerously low. The Italian army suffered a high number of casualties. Of an army of five million, 600,000 men were killed. Many of the soldiers barely understood why they were fighting at all. The losses seemed a pointless waste.

Tension in the cities

The mood in Italian cities grew ugly. Italian industry had expanded rapidly between 1915 and 1918. But the workers endured great hardship. The government imposed harsh discipline in the arms factories. Food shortages led to serious riots in late 1917. The next year, even though there was more food, tension between classes persisted.

At the end of the war Italy was racked by social and political turmoil. Victory strengthened the cause of the nationalists, who had argued for Italy joining the war back in 1915. At the same time, economic problems made the position of the socialists and the communists stronger. The old liberal elite appeared weak. And they would lose more face when they failed to gain territorial concessions from the Allies after the war. It seemed that the Italians had suffered a great deal for very little.

HOME FRONT
Italy

Italian women munitions workers holding 18-pounder shells at a railhead dump.

Kiel MUTINY

Germany's naval commanders wanted a final battle against the British fleet, even though it would probably bring defeat. The German sailors refused to obey their orders.

On October 27, 1918, Admiral Rheinhard Scheer, chief of the German naval staff, ordered the High Seas Fleet into the North Sea. The fleet had played little part in the war so far. The British Royal Navy had kept it largely confined to port. Now Scheer wanted to attack the British. To fight one last, heroic sea battle was a matter of honor.

The crews thought differently. For two years they had been complaining about their rations and working conditions. Tensions had risen between the sailors and their officers. Now they came to a head. The seamen refused to take part in what they saw as a suicide mission.

Five times Scheer gave the order to put to sea; five times the men ignored him. Crews at sea extinguished their ships' boilers. Sailors on leave refused to return to their bases. At the bases sailors chanted: "We do not put to sea. For us the war is

Striking German sailors on board a warship at Kiel, November 5, 1918.

A group of German soldiers and armed civilians during the uprising at Kiel, November 1918.

over." They called for an end to the Hohenzollern monarchy and the creation of a socialist republic.

On November 3 around 3,000 sailors and workers raised the communist Red Flag at Kiel, on the Baltic Sea. The revolt gathered pace. Next day thousands of factory workers and 20,000 troops joined the uprising. Naval commanders fled for their lives. Soon the revolt spread to other German cities. The unrest, coupled with crippling defeats on the Western Front, would finally force Germany's leaders to bring the war to an end.

EYEWITNESS

Seaman Richard Stumpf, who served in the German High Seas Fleet, witnessed the naval mutiny of October 1918 at first hand. He gave an account in his diary of the initial stages of the mutiny at Wilhelmshaven, and recalled that it was suppressed. This action failed, however, to prevent the rebellion from spreading.

66 On the *Thüringen*, the former model ship of the fleet, the mutiny was at its worst. The crew simply locked up the petty officers and refused to weigh anchor. The men told the captain that they would only fight against the English if their fleet appeared in German waters. They no longer wanted to risk their lives uselessly. Six destroyers and a submarine were summoned, and aimed their guns at the ship. A company of naval infantry then occupied all the compartments and arrested three hundred men. Reports of similar happenings came from the *Helgoland*. 99

WHERE TO FIND...
Revolution in Berlin: 7:108
Defeat of the German Army: 7:94
Armistice: 7:112

Economic Breakdown

Like the other countries involved in the fighting, Germany had not planned for a long war when it began in 1914. Because the country depended on imported foods and raw materials, it soon became vulnerable to economic warfare. Britain's naval blockade meant that by the final year of the war, the Germans were suffering terrible economic problems.

Both food and consumer goods, such as furniture, were in short supply, so the prices of both rose steeply. People's wages were worth less than before. And the government's way of raising taxes – by adding them onto the cost of goods, rather than taking them out of people's wages – meant that poor people had to pay a much higher proportion of their income than the rich.

Ordinary Germans sensed that the burdens of war were not being shared equally. Employers and war profiteers, unlike most of the population, continued to enjoy a high standard of living; many actually saw their incomes increase during the war. This led to growing resentment between Ger-

German men and women line up in the street for food.

many's different classes. The split, in turn, undermined the spirit of national unity that was vital in wartime.

After 1916 units of the German army kept a close watch on the mood of the people. These Home Front Regional Commands noted the growing resentment of the poor toward the rich. Their reports spelled out that it was not shortages of goods that made people most angry; it was the unfair way they were distributed.

After around 1916 war-weariness became permanent among the poorer people in German society. Although morale rose or fell according to the news from the battlefront, there was a constant undercurrent of rebellion. Food riots broke out from time to time, usually during the winter months rather than after the harvest in early autumn.

The number of strikes in German industry also began to rise, providing another sign of growing unrest. In the last 18 months of the war strikes became an almost daily occurrence. In January 1918, for example, strikes in Berlin and other German cities were supported by more than a million people. Such labor disputes stopped industrial production and so damaged the war effort. One of the major reasons for the German army's eventual defeat on the Western Front in the autumn of 1918 was that Germany simply could not match the number of guns, tanks,

One of the many railroad installations in the German mining area which was brought to a halt by strike action.

and aircraft being produced by the Allies' factories.

The national unity with which Germany had entered the war in 1914 had broken down under social and economic strains. On the home front social tensions had reached dangerous levels, as an army report on the central city of Magdeburg showed: "The previous large gulf between rich and poor, which had largely been closed in the early days of the war, now continues to widen, the more the longer. Among the poorer sections of the population a pernicious hatred against the rich and so-called war profiteers has built up, which one can only hope will not lead to a terrible explosion."

REVOLUTION IN BERLIN

Defeat in battle was followed by uprising at home. The Kaiser abdicated, and the new German republic sought peace.

This group of "revolutionaries" is pictured in Unter den Linden, Berlin's most famous street. The workers' and soldiers' councils that sprang up in German cities in November 1918 quickly distributed arms to their supporters, but their aims were less revolutionary than the government feared.

By October 1918 it was clear that Germany would lose the war. The spirit of the German people collapsed. They had made many sacrifices in the hope of victory. Now every report from the front told of defeats. Germany's allies were giving up. Politicians and the German people all wanted the war to be over.

For more than a year regular strikes had been called to protest food shortages and working conditions. Now the strikes took on a more political tone. The workers called for peace but also demanded political reform and the end of the monarchy. Even the middle classes and the army leaders who had supported the war were demoralized because they knew Germany could not win. They worried about what would happen after the end of the conflict. They wanted to head off a communist revolution in Germany which would bring changes similar to those the Bolshevik revolutionaries were making in the Russia.

The Kaiser abdicates

In October 1918 the Kaiser agreed to make Germany a constitutional monarchy like Britain. It would still have a ruler, but the government would have to answer to an elected parliament. The Kaiser's gesture offered too little too late. For years Germans had been frustrated by the government's failure to make genuine political reforms. And they were bitter that ordinary people, rather than the privileged classes, had shouldered the burdens of war.

After the sailors' mutiny at Kiel on November 3 came the establishment of revolutionary councils in many other cities. The troops at the front were also rebellious. General Gröner, the new deputy chief of staff, warned that the situation was desperate. The fleet would not obey orders, revolution was imminent, and troops refused to fire on the revolutionaries.

By the end of the first week of November the revolutionary mood had spread to the capital, Berlin. Crowds called for the Kaiser to give up his throne. Wilhelm at first refused. He wanted to bring troops back from the front to crush the uprising at home. The generals convinced him this would not work, and he agreed to go into exile. He abdicated on November 9 and fled across the border to neutral Holland.

In Berlin, meanwhile, several groups competed to form the new government. The extreme left-wing Spartacus League seized the Imperial Palace. From the palace balcony Karl Liebknecht, one of the movement's leaders, proclaimed the establishment of a Bolshevik-style German Soviet Republic. At the same time, the moderate socialist party, the Social Democrats, announced the formation of an alternative German republic.

The Gröner-Ebert pact

That same day Prince Max of Baden, the last chancellor of the German empire, handed over power to Friedrich Ebert, the Social Democrat leader. That evening General Gröner telephoned Ebert to offer him the army's support if he needed it to put down the Spartacists. Ebert accepted.

On November 9, 1918, the Kaiser and his personal staff wait on a station platform while Dutch authorities decide whether to allow him to go into exile in Holland.

The army leadership had done well from the upheaval. Now the new government, rather than the generals, would negotiate and sign the armistice that would have to be agreed with the Allies – and take the blame for its shortcomings in the eyes of the German public.

Ebert and Gröner's deal committed the socialists and the army – who were not natural allies – to working together to stop something neither side wanted: a communist takeover. Ebert might not actually have required military support. He was more worried than he needed to be about the communist threat. The workers' and soldiers' councils did contain extremist elements, but the vast majority of their members supported moderate reforms.

alternatives

What if the Spartacist revolt in Berlin had succeeded? They might have captured other cities. But their success would only have been brief. The Allies would not tolerate a communist regime in Germany so soon after the Russian Revolution. They would probably have used troops to suppress it. The communists would also have faced opposition from most Germans: the middle classes, country dwellers, industrialists, and the army. If civil war had come, the communists would probably have lost.

Government supporters defend a barricade in a Berlin street during the Spartacist uprising, a left-wing attempt to seize power, in January 1919.

politics

Rosa Luxemburg
and the Spartacus League

Rosa Luxemburg (1871–1919) was born in Poland to Jewish parents. She became a communist in 1890 and helped found the Polish Communist Party. In 1899 she moved to Berlin and became prominent in the German Social Democratic Party, known as the SPD.

Luxemburg was an important political thinker who believed that change would come only through revolution. Although the SPD supported the war, she opposed it. She left the party and together with others, including Karl Liebknecht, began her own party. The *Spartakusbund*, or Spartacus League, aimed at ending the war through revolution and the establishment of a proletarian, or workers', government. Because of her views Luxemburg spent most of the war in prison, though she was released on November 9, 1918. The following month she spoke at a Congress of Workers' Councils in Berlin which called for the abolition of the army and its replacement by a militia – an armed body of citizens normally used only in emergencies. Chancellor Ebert, supported by the army commanders, rejected this.

In January 1919 the Spartacists tried to seize power in Berlin. The uprising was crushed by government troops. Both Liebknecht and Luxemburg were killed. The suppression of the revolt led to a rift between the communists and the Social Democrats in Germany. Later the two parties did not work together against the right-wing Nazi extremists. The lack of a united opposition was one of the reasons Adolf Hitler was able to rise to become Germany's dictator in the 1930s.

Rosa Luxemburg addressing a socialist meeting in Stuttgart before the war.

WHERE TO FIND...

Defeat of the German Army: 7:94

Armistice: 7:112

October Revolution: 6:100

Kiel Mutiny: 7:104

Prince Max of Baden: 5:19

Gröner: 4:94

Postwar World: Germany: 8:66

American troops in a damaged church on November 11, 1918

ARMISTICE

Faced with defeat, Germany's military commanders had little choice but to agree to the Allies' demands to end the war. The Armistice went into force on November 11, 1918.

O n September 28, 1918, the German government made a tentative request for an armistice to U.S. President Woodrow Wilson. The approach began a series of negotiations that would lead to an end to the fighting.

German second thoughts

The Allies had pushed back the Germans on the Western Front during August and September. Germany lacked the men and the resources to fight back. Its allies were retreating on every front. At the end of September Bulgaria agreed to an armistice with the Allies.

During the first week of October 1918, however, the Allied offensives slowed. The mood of the Germans and Austrians changed. The "Peace Note" they sent to Wilson on October 4 did not sound as though it came from the defeated side in the war. It refused to accept any Allied terms harmful to Germany or Austria.

President Wilson replied on October 8. He repeated the conditions included in the Fourteen Points in which he had outlined America's war aims in 1917. The war would not end until German troops had left Belgium and France, and other European peoples had been allowed to decide

EYEWITNESS

Amos N. Wilder recalled that he, and many of the troops in his detachment, were too tired to celebrate the end of the war. Others were more boisterous:

66 Our bunch wasn't particularly demonstrative, tho' they understood well it meant peace. They kept remarking for the next few hours and days how strange the absolute silence on the horizon was … It was told us by the Marines and infantry that the Germans were a lot more tickled than we were. They threw down their gas masks, helmets, etc. Some were seen in the tops of trees from our side of the Meuse brandishing their guns and shouting gleefully in our direction. Some Americans had bonfires the night of the 11th and 12th and let off their spirits with hand grenades and 'potato-mashers.' 99

their own political future. This meant, in effect, that the Austro-Hungarian empire would break up into a series of independent states. Germany would have to give up territory to France in Alsace-Lorraine and perhaps in the east to the Poles.

Some realists, such as the new German chancellor, Prince Max of Baden, were prepared to consider Wilson's terms. The military was less willing to give up territory. It planned to continue fighting. But the end of October brought a change. General Ludendorff was forced to resign.

In late October, too, the Austrian empire began to disintegrate, as its subject peoples declared their independence. The Austrian army was losing in Italy and Serbia. Emperor Karl requested an armistice, which went into effect on November 4. The Turks were already out of the war. Germany was isolated abroad; at home it was in the midst of a revolution, and the Kaiser was about to abdicate.

The generals set their terms

An armistice is not the same thing as a peace treaty. An armistice is only an agreement to stop fighting for the time being,

rather than an official end to war. In theory fighting could start again, so in October the Allied leaders asked their top generals for advice on what terms the armistice should include. The French commanders Foch and Pétain, the American Pershing, and the British Haig had one common aim. They wanted to make it absolutely impossible for Germany to start fighting again if peace negotiations failed.

The generals could not agree how to do this. Pershing wanted to continue the war

A British officer and his men welcome the news that the fighting is over. Some Allied soldiers celebrated the armistice, but others were too tired and saddened by the long struggle to take much joy from the occasion.

A crowd waits for
definite news of the
armistice outside the
White House in
Washington, D.C..
Some American
newspapers reported
that the armistice had
been agreed some
days before it actually
took place.

until Germany was even more decisively beaten than it was already. But Foch was confident that the Allies could already impose harsh terms. "I am not waging war for the sake of waging war," he said. "If I obtain through the armistice the conditions that we wish to impose upon Germany, I am satisfied. Once this object is attained, nobody has the right to shed one drop more of blood."

The railroad car

On the morning of November 9 German negotiators arrived to meet Foch. For security reasons the French general did not meet them at his headquarters. Instead they boarded a train which took them to an isolated clearing in the middle of a forest about 40 miles northeast of Paris. An identical train waited there on a parallel track. On board were Foch himself, along with other French and British officers.

The Germans crossed the clearing to Foch's train on duckboards which had

been laid across the clearing. They entered an old dining car which had been converted into an office, with a long table around which the four delegates from each side would sit.

The Germans were in a weak position. The revolution in Germany had spread to Berlin; many Germans were starving. German troops were deserting in growing numbers on the Western Front. The Germans had no choice but to agree to all the Allies' terms.

The Germans agreed to hand over thousands of guns, machine guns, artillery pieces, aircraft, railroad engines, and wagons, all their submarines, and many of their battleships. They promised to evacuate all occupied territories and allow Allied troops into Germany. The Allied blockade of Germany would stay in effect until a peace settlement was signed. The Armistice was to go into effect on Monday, November 11, at 11:00 a.m., the 11th hour of the 11th day of the 11th month.

behind the lines

The death of Wilfred Owen

On November 4, 1918, the British poet Wilfred Owen (1893–1918) died on the Western Front. An infantry officer, Owen was leading an attack across a canal when he was hit by German fire. His parents learned of their son's death seven days later, on Armistice Day.

Owen, like many others, had joined up enthusiastically in the early days of the fighting. However, he became increasingly disillusioned by the horror, cruelty, and waste of war. He had begun writing poetry before 1914 and now vividly expressed his sentiments about the conflict through his writing. He gained greater confidence as a poet after meeting his fellow British officer and poet, Siegfried Sassoon, while both men were recovering from "shell shock" at a hospital in 1917. In the last year of his life the war inspired Owen to write many of his greatest poems.

In a letter to his mother shortly before his death Owen explained his decision to return to the Western Front after his time in the hospital. He wanted, he said, to help his men, both on the battlefield and through his poetry: "I came out in order to help these boys; directly, by leading them as well as an officer can; indirectly, by watching their sufferings that I may speak of them as well as a pleader can."

In October Owen was frustrated by the Allies' reluctance to accept the Germans' initial requests for an armistice. He was cynical about rumors that Austria had asked for an end to the war: "The new soldiers cheer when they hear these rumors, but the old ones bite their pipes, and go on cleaning their rifles, unbelieving." When Owen died, he left a draft of his first book of poems. In the introduction he wrote: "My subject is war, and the pity of war." Siegfried Sassoon published the book in 1920. The evocative poems give a penetrating insight into the horror of trench warfare and the feelings of the soldiers.

Wilfred Owen.

WHERE TO FIND...

Defeat of the German Army: 7:94

Wilson's 14 Points: 7:10

Ludendorff Resigns: 7:94

Reactions to the Armistice: 7:116

Reactions to the Armistice: JOY AND SADNESS

Wild parties followed the news of the Armistice in every Allied city, but too many families had lost loved ones for it to be an entirely happy occasion.

News of the Armistice caused jubilation throughout the Allied countries. In Washington, DC, crowds gathered outside the White House. In New York ticker tape rained down in Wall Street, and celebrations began in Times Square. Department stores cashed in by holding "Victory Sales."

In London hundreds of thousands of people rushed into the streets. One observer described the cheering of the crowds as "the wild noise of a world released from nightmare." In the French capital, Paris, there was a similar explosion of joy. An eyewitness noted, "In the course of the morning the guns started firing, and Paris went charmingly off her head. Along the boulevards processions at once formed... the whole city resounds with cheers."

In the defeated capitals – Berlin and Vienna – the mood was far more somber. The people were worried less about defeat than about surviving. They faced food shortages and political uncertainty.

French cavalry parade in the German town of Wiesbaden after the Armistice. They and other Allied troops were to occupy parts of Germany until a peace treaty was made. The expressions of the German onlookers show that they resented this foreign occupation of their country.

Even in the Allied countries, however, the victory celebrations were short-lived. Too many people had lost sons, brothers, fathers, husbands, and lovers in the carnage of the war. People celebrated for a short time, but the overwhelming sense of grief and loss remained.

On the battlefronts the emotions were also mixed. Troops were relieved no longer to fear death or wounds, but they also thought of their fallen comrades. A British soldier asked his sergeant what an armistice was, since he did not know what the word meant. The sergeant spoke for many when he replied, "Time to bury the dead."

On the German side some soldiers felt betrayed by those who had signed the Armistice. They believed they had not lost the war, but that the politicians and the revolutionaries at home had wasted their sacrifices and handed victory to the Allies at the negotiating table.

EYEWITNESS

The Chicago Tribune reported that the end of the war was celebrated in a festive atmosphere in that city:

❝ Harlequins danced beneath the street lamps in the arms of pretty girls dressed as men. Uncle Sam strode with dignity beside an uproarious Charlie Chaplin. Girls wore short trousers of boys, long ones of men, and one was seen in the full regalia of an army officer. Men jammed their way through the crowds which inverted waste baskets over their heads to protect their hats from the sticks and stones of men and women revelers who lined the walls of buildings. Hundreds of overloaded men reeled along the streets beside women reeling with hysteria. ❞

WHERE TO FIND...

Armistice: 7:112
Cost of the War:
  8:10

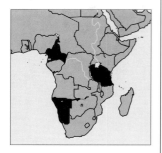

The War in AFRICA

The Allies captured most German colonies early in the war but German forces in eastern Africa held out to the end.

Nigerian and British troops pursuing Lettow-Vorbeck's army trek through East Africa. Supplies for the armies in Africa usually had to be transported long distances on foot or by pack animals.

Between 1915 and 1918 hundreds of thousands of Allied troops were deployed in Africa against the few thousand German and native troops defending Germany's colonies.

The Allies had easily captured the German colony of Togoland in 1914. But German forces continued to fight in Cam-

eroon, German Southwest Africa – today called Namibia – and in and around German East Africa, or modern Tanzania.

Cameroon

In Cameroon the Allies had to contend with bad roads, baking heat, torrential rain, and rampant disease. When they finally

reached the colonial capital, Yaoundé, most of the enemy had already fled to neighboring Spanish Guinea, which was neutral. Although the Germans never had more than 8,000 men defending Cameroon, they managed to keep 64,000 Allied troops occupied until February 1916.

German Southwest Africa

The South Africans were also involved in Allied fighting during 1915. Thirty-five thousand troops attacked German Southwest Africa defeating the Germans at Keetmanshoop and Gibeon in April. Meanwhile a further 20,000 men under the command of the prime minister, General Louis Botha, forged their way to the colonial capital of Windhoek. Despite the fact that 6,000 Germans waged a determined

and effective guerrilla campaign, Botha's troops occupied Windhoek in May. The last of the defending Germans finally capitulated on July 9, 1915.

German East Africa

In German East Africa, Colonel Paul von Lettow-Vorbeck had successfully beaten off British attacks in 1914. By 1916, however, the Allies had assembled seemingly overwhelming forces against him.

In early 1916 South African General Jan Smuts led an advance south from British East Africa, now known as Kenya. Belgian and British troops marched southeast from the Congo, modern Zaire, and more British moved north from Northern Rhodesia, today called Zambia. But Lettow-Vorbeck excelled at guerrilla warfare and Smuts found it difficult to pin his enemy down.

In 1917 the Allies did manage to take Mahenge, the site of a major German base, but many enemy troops escaped. The Germans marched south into Portuguese East Africa – now Mozambique – where the native population helped them with supplies. The pursuing armies forced the Germans to march on. The campaign continued into 1918 with the Germans still raiding and ambushing the Allied columns. Lettow-Vorbeck and his last 150 Germans and 3,000 native troops eventually surrendered in Northern Rhodesia on November 23, 1918, as soon as they heard about the armistice agreed in Europe 12 days before.

Lettow-Vorbeck had managed to keep over 370,000 Allied troops away from the main war fronts, even though he never had more than 15,000 men. Although it had to end in defeat, his campaign could not have done more for Germany

WHERE TO FIND...

Colonial War: 2:42
Boer Revolt: 2:70
German East Africa: 2:102

SET INDEX

Index of BIOGRAPHIES

Picture credits

GLOSSARY

artillery barrage – a heavy bombardment of explosive shells onto enemy positions, often used to prepare for an infantry attack.

bayonet – a sharp blade attached to the muzzle of a rifle and used for hand-to-hand fighting.

blockade – the use of warships and mines to cut off an enemy's sea trade.

chief of staff – the military head of an army.

depth charge – a waterproof explosive that detonates underwater to destroy enemy submarines.

division – a military unit of between 10,000 and 17,000 soldiers and support troops.

draft – large-scale selection of civilians for compulsory military service.

fortress – a large, heavily defended permanent fortification, often surrounding a town or city.

grenade – a small missile containing explosives or chemicals, such as poison gas or a smoke producer.

home front – the wartime activity of civilians away from the battle fronts.

infantry – a branch of an army trained and equipped to fight and move on foot.

intelligence – information about enemy positions and plans.

land mine – an explosive charge that is buried just beneath the surface of the ground. The land mine explodes if a person stands on it or if a tank drives over the top.

mobilization – the assembly and preparation of a country's armed forces for war.

mortar – a short, portable artillery weapon that fires heavy shells in an arc over short distances.

No Man's Land – the ground between the trenches of opposing forces.

"over the top" – the name given to climbing out of one's own trenches to advance.

propaganda – information designed to influence public opinion or damage enemy morale.

reconnaissance – a survey of enemy territory to gather intelligence.

reparations – payments made by a defeated nation in compensation for costs and damages sustained during war.

reserves – a body of troops which is held back from action for later use.

salient – an outward bulge in an army's front line which has to be defended on three exposed sides.

sea mine – a waterproof explosive charge that is placed on or beneath the surface of the water. The mine explodes if a vessel touches it or passes near by.

shell shock – a psychological trauma suffered by soldiers under prolonged enemy fire.

shrapnel – flying fragments of a bomb, mine, or shell that can cause serious or fatal injuries.

stormtroops – soldiers trained and armed to break through enemy lines after an artillery barrage.

strategic bombing – air raids designed to damage an enemy's military, economic, or industrial capacity.

theater of war – an area of land, sea, or air that is directly involved in military actions.

trenches – long, deep ditches dug in the ground for use as defensive fortifications.

trench foot – an infection of the feet caused by cold and wet trench conditions.

U-boat – a term for German and Austrian submarines. The word comes from the German *Unterseeboot*, meaning "submarine."

Zeppelin – a rigid airship constructed of a frame covered by material and filled with gas.

BIBLIOGRAPHY

History

Brogan, Hugh, *The Pelican History of the United States of America.* New York: Penguin USA, 1987.

Bruce, Anthony, *An Illustrated Companion to the First World War.* New York: Penguin USA, 1990.

Gilbert, Martin, *First World War.* New York: Henry Holt & Co., 1996.

Gilbert, Martin, *Atlas of the First World War.* New York: Oxford University Press, 1994.

Gray, Randal, and Christopher Argyle, eds., *Chronicle of the First World War,* 2 vols. Mechanicsburg, PA: Stackpole, 1991.

Joll, James, *The Origins of the First World War.* New York: Longman, 1984.

Joll, James, *Europe Since 1870: An International History.* New York: HarperCollins College Publishers.

MacDonald, Lyn, *1914–1918: Voices and Images of the Great War.* New York: Penguin USA, 1991.

Macksey, Kenneth, *The Penguin Encyclopedia of Weapons & Military Technology from Pre-History to the Present Day.* New York: Penguin USA, 1994.

Pope, Stephen, and Wheal, Elizabeth-Anne, *Dictionary of the First World War.* New York: St. Martin's Press, 1995.

Reed, John Silas, *Ten Days that Shook the World.* New York: Bantam, 1992.

Thomas, Gill, *Life on All Fronts: Women in the First World War.* New York: Cambridge University Press, 1989.

Tuchmann, Barbara W., *The Guns of August.* New York: Ballantine, 1994.

Weintraub, Stanley, *A Stillness Heard Round the World. The End of the Great War: November 1918.* New York: Oxford University Press, 1987.

Winter, Denis, *Death's Men: Soldiers of the Great War.* New York: Penguin USA, 1985.

Winter, Jay, *The Great War.* New York: Penguin USA, 1996.

Fiction, Memoirs, and Poetry

Brittain, Vera, *A Testament of Youth.* New York: Viking, 1994.

Brown, Malcolm, *The Imperial War Museum Book of the First World War: A Great Conflict Recalled in Previously Unpublished Letters, Diaries & Memoirs.* Philadelphia: Trans-Atlantic Publications Inc., 1993.

Dos Passos, John, *1919.* New York: Amereon Ltd.

Faulkner, William, *A Soldier's Pay.* New York: Liveright, 1990.

Graves, Robert, *Goodbye to All That.* Providence, RI: Berghahn Books, 1995.

Hašek, Jaroslav, *The Good Soldier Švejk.* New York: Robert Bentley Publishing, 1980.

Hemingway, Ernest, *A Farewell to Arms.* New York: Simon & Schuster, 1995.

MacArthur, Douglas, *Reminiscences.* New York: Da Capo, 1985.

Remarque, Erich Maria, *All Quiet on the Western Front.* New York: Barron, 1984.

Sassoon, Siegfried, *Collected Poems, 1908–1953.* Winchester, MA: Faber & Faber.

Sassoon, Siegfried, *Memoirs of an Infantry Officer.* Winchester, MA: Faber & Faber, 1965.

Solzhenitsyn, Aleksandr, *August 1914.* New York: Farrar, Strauss & Giroux Inc, 1989.

Owen, Wilfred, *Collected Poems.* New York: New Directions, 1964.

Vaughan, Edwin, *Some Desperate Glory.* New York: Henry Holt & Co., 1988

Wilder, Amos N., *Armageddon Revisited. A World War I Journal.* New Haven, CT: Yale University Press, 1994.

Yeats, W.B., *The Collected Poems.* New York: Simon and Schuster, 1996.